that
reminds
me
of a
joke

D1009796

that reminds me of a joke

Andy Simmons

Humor Editor for
Reader's Digest Magazine

Outrageous News Stories That Echo Our Favorite Jokes

Reader's
digest

The Reader's Digest Association, Inc. • New York, NY/Montreal

a reader's digest book

Cover design: George McKeon
Illustrations: Gary Hovland

Library of Congress Cataloging-in-Publication Data
Simmons, Andy.
  That reminds me of a joke : outrageous news stories that echo our
favorite jokes / Andy Simmons ; illustrated by Gary Hovland.
     pages cm
  Summary: "A humorous book that pairs brief, funny news stories with
jokes that are eerily familiar"-- Provided by publisher.
  ISBN 978-1-62145-217-1 (paperback) -- ISBN 978-1-62145-218-8 (epub) 1.
 Newspapers--Headlines--Humor. 2. Online journalsim--Humor. 3.
American wit and humor. I. Title.
  PN6231.N63S66 2015
  818'.60208--dc23

                              2014045962

We are committed to both the quality of our products and the
service we provide to our customers. We value your comments,
so please feel free to contact us.

            The Reader's Digest Association
            Adult Trade Publishing
            44 S. Broadway
            White Plains, NY 10601

For more Reader's Digest products and information,
visit our website:
            www.rd.com (in the United States)
            www.readersdigest.ca (in Canada)

Printed in China

1 3 5 7 9 10 8 6 4 2

contents

introduction

I don't know about you, but I go through life constantly being reminded of jokes. No matter what the situation, a joke invariably pops into my little pea-brain, crowding out whatever it is I should be paying attention to at the time. For example, a few days ago I was walking my two dogs. As one of them stopped to (how do I put this delicately) polish a fire hydrant, this gag came to mind: "Two dogs are walking down the street. One says, 'Wait a minute,' and then crosses the road. He sniffs around a fire hydrant and returns. The other dog says, 'What was that all about?' The first dog replies, 'Just checking my messages.'"

Of course, it's not just my personal life. The news is a font of gag-worthy events. There's not a day that goes by that I don't scan the headlines or scroll through news feeds and find myself cracking up at the jokes they suggest. Dumb criminals, cowardly politicians, spiteful spouses, and hilarious gags? Can't beat that combo. Which is what impelled me to go to the powers that be at *Reader's Digest* and suggest that I write this book. Which, of course, reminded me of a joke . . .

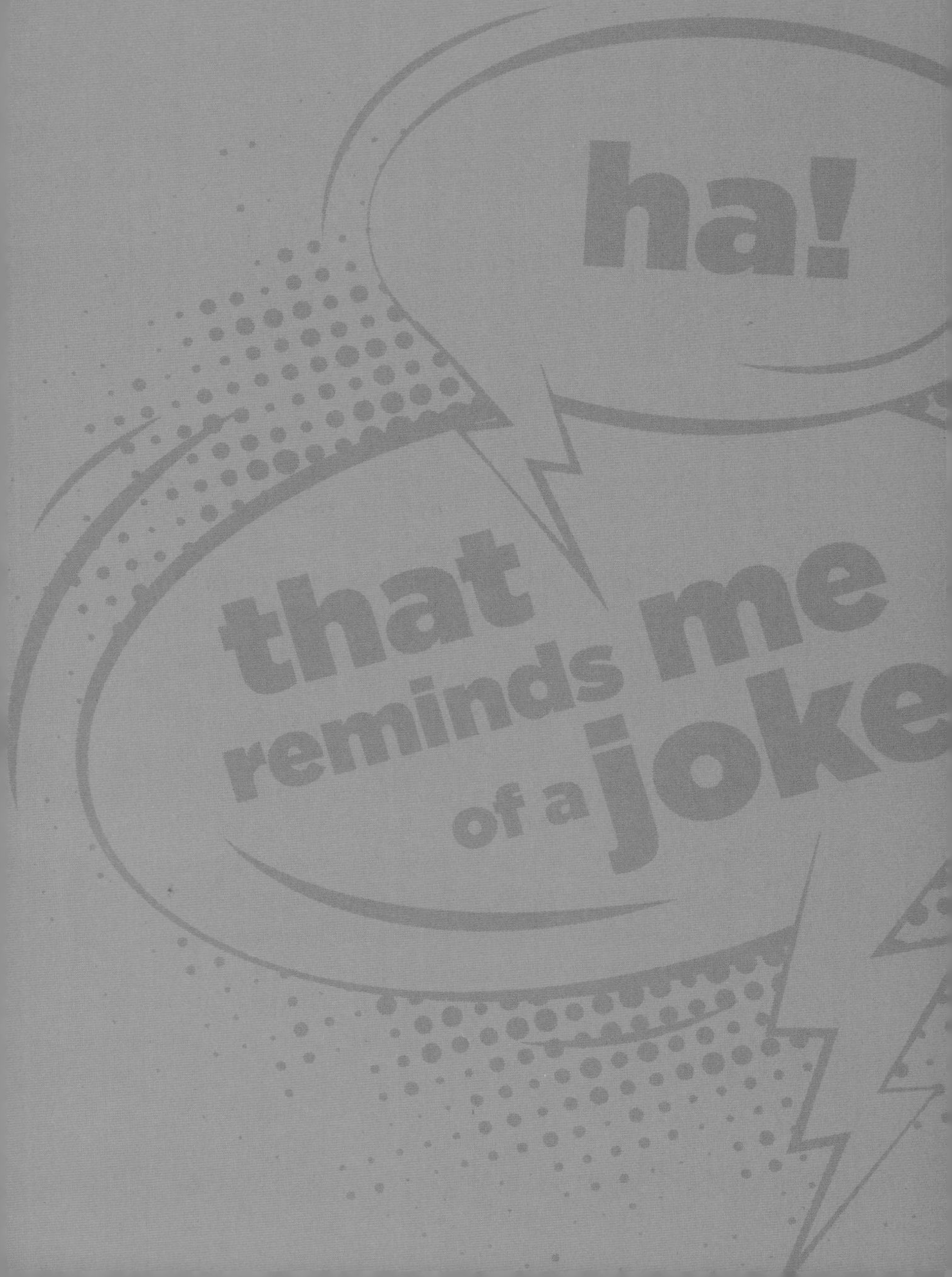
ha!
that reminds me of a joke

love

and marriage and a baby carriage

"The other night I ate at a real nice family restaurant. Every table had an argument going on."

—George Carlin

In All Fairness, It Was a Very Nice Hotel

A husband in Kenya told his wife that he needed to travel to his home village to visit family, but instead he rented a hotel room with his mistress. Later that evening, he stepped out into the hallway to call his wife. At that moment, the door to the next room opened and his wife walked out answering his call. No, it wasn't a trap—inside her room was the man *she* had been having an affair with.

Source: standardmedia.co.ke

 ## That Reminds Me of a Joke

"I'm going to get a divorce," Jennifer told Dana. "Yesterday, I saw my husband going to the movies with another woman."

"There could be a perfectly good explanation," said Dana. "Why didn't you follow them into the theater?"

"I couldn't. The guy I was with had already seen the movie."

▮ ▮

But She Has a Great Personality

President Ian Khama of Botswana is looking for a wife, but only slim, beautiful women need apply. Pointing to a heavyset government official, Khama said, "I don't want one like her. She may fail to pass through the door, break furniture with her heavy weight, and even break the vehicle's shock absorber."

Source: ABC News

That Reminds Me of a Joke

A husband and wife are shopping in the supermarket. The husband picks up a case of Budweiser and puts it in their shopping cart.

"What do you think you're doing?" asks the wife.

"They're on sale, only $10 for 24 cans," he replies.

"Put them back, we can't afford them," demands the wife.

A few minutes later, in another aisle, the woman picks up a $20 jar of face cream and puts it in the shopping cart.

"What do you think you're doing?" asks the husband.

"It's my face cream. It makes me look beautiful," replies the wife.

"So does 24 cans of Budweiser, and it's half the price."

A Whole Lot of Love

Last July, Richard Barton Jr., of Grand Rapids, Michigan, got married and posted the photos on Facebook. One of the people viewing the pictures was Barton's first wife, who decided to call the cops. Why? She says she was still his wife because they were separated but never divorced. Barton, who claims he signed divorce papers, was arrested on charges of polygamy.

Source: mlive.com

 That Reminds Me of a Joke

Having more than one wife is called polygamy. Having only one wife is called monotony.

▪ ▪

Shh! It's Classified

A classified ad found in the Richmond (Virginia) *Times-Dispatch:* Wedding band—Ladies size 5, gold, 5 diamonds, $250. Worn only 32 days by an old, narcissistic witch.

 That Reminds Me of a Joke

Why is divorce so expensive? Because it's worth it.

▪ ▪

I've Got the Toy, the Car Seat . . . What Am I Forgetting?

Philadelphia jewel thieves grabbed thousands of dollars in valuables. But they exited the store forgetting something: their four-year-old son.

Source: philly.com

That Reminds Me of a Joke

A lawyer visits his client in jail. "I've got good news and bad news," he says.

"Give me the bad news first," says the prisoner.

"Your blood was found at the scene of the crime," replies the lawyer.

"So what's the good news?" asks the prisoner.

"Your cholesterol is quite low."

Bonus Joke

While sightseeing at George Washington's home in Mount Vernon, Virginia, a family friend became nervous when she thought she had lost two of my cousins. She looked everywhere and called out their names repeatedly. Soon our friend grew perturbed that not one of the Mount Vernon employees had joined in the search. Instead, they simply stood around, staring at her as if she were crazy. Finally, just a few moments later, my cousins—George and Martha—came out from hiding.

—Tracy Nelson

911? This Is an Emergency. I Need an Excuse!

A Brooklyn, New York, man was found on the street with his hands, mouth and legs tied up with duct tape. The victim claimed that two men had abducted him a couple of weeks earlier, then dumped him on the street. His story unraveled, however, when cops began to wonder why the roll of duct tape was dangling from his wrist. That's when the man fessed up: He'd staged the kidnapping because he was too scared to explain his absence to his girlfriend.

Source: The *New York Post*

That Reminds Me of a Joke

A husband goes out drinking on Friday night and ends up having way too much fun. When he eventually sobers up, it's Sunday afternoon. He struggles to come up with a good explanation for his wife, then lands on an idea. He sneaks back into his house, and calls his home phone. As his wife goes to pick it up, he shouts, "Honey! Don't pay the ransom! I've escaped!"

There Are Just Some Things You Shouldn't Ask a Kid

A student from Poland called the cops on his mother, saying she was guilty of psychological torture. Her offense: asking him to take a bath and clean his room.

Source: *Ananova*

 ## That Reminds Me of a Joke

Two psychotherapists pass each other in the hallway. The first says to the second, "Hello!"

The second smiles back nervously and half nods his head. When he is comfortably out of earshot, he mumbles, "I wonder what *that* was all about?"

Wedded Blitz

An Australian man whose wife cheated on him with his best friend has put her wedding dress up for sale. "Due to be married soon? Not planning on staying faithful? Then THIS is the wedding dress for you!" read his online ad. It continued: "A one-of-a-kind garment designed by Benedict Arnold, believed to be derived from the very cloth Judas Iscariot himself wore to the Garden of Gethsemane to betray the only son of God—Jesus Christ."

Since being posted, the ad has had 200,000 visits.

Source: web.orange.co.uk

That Reminds Me of a Joke

A guy tells his psychiatrist: "It was terrible. I was at the airport about to leave on a business trip when my flight was canceled, so I texted my wife that I was coming home. When I arrived at my house, I found her in the arms of my best friend. I don't get it. How could she do this to me?"

"Well," says the psychiatrist. "Maybe she didn't get your text."

It'll Be Settled at the My-Lawyer-Is-Better-Than-Yours Court House

After learning that her husband was cheating on her, a British woman let her husband know she was leaving him by convincing the owner of her favorite pub to change its name temporarily to "Paul, I Am Divorcing You."

Source: mirror.co.uk

That Reminds Me of a Joke

Kathy goes to her local bank, walks into the manager's office, and says, "I want a loan; I'm going to divorce my husband."

"Oh, we don't give loans for divorces," the manager says. "We offer loans only for things like real estate, appliances, automobiles, businesses, and home improvement."

Kathy interrupts, "Stop right there. This definitely falls into the category of home improvement."

I I I I I I I I I I I I I I I I I I I I I I I I I I I I I I I I I I I I I I I I I I I I I I

Please Excuse Johnnie, He Has Me for a Parent

What's the most entertaining part of the day for a teacher? Reading the notes from parents for why their kids missed school.

- "My son was absent yesterday because he had a sore trout."
- "John has been absent because he had two teeth taken off his face."
- "My daughter was absent yesterday because she was tired. She spent this weekend with the marines."

Source: School-survival.net

That Reminds Me of a Joke

Pupil (on phone): My son has a bad cold and won't be able to come to school today.

School Secretary: Who is this?

Pupil: This is my father speaking.

Sweet Justice!

A Facebook mom teaches her son a lesson on manners: Hi, this is XXXXX's mom. I wanted to let all of you know that he is no longer allowed on Facebook due to choices he made today. He posted on Facebook personal information about someone that, regardless if it were true or not, was rude. Because he chose to try and make her mad by spreading personal information, I thought he should know how it feels when the tables are turned. He wet the bed until he was eight.

From blameitonthevoices.com

That Reminds Me of a Joke

Late one Saturday night, a woman was awakened by her phone. "Hello," she said.

A breathless voice on the line rushed into a lengthy speech. "Mom, this is Tony. I'm sorry I woke you up, but I had to call because I'm going to be a little late getting home because Dad's car got a flat tire, but it's not my fault. Honest! I don't know what happened. The tire just went flat while we were in the movie. Please don't be angry, okay?"

Since the woman didn't have a son, she knew it was a wrong number. "I'm sorry, dear, but you must have misdialed. I don't have a son."

There was a long pause, "Gosh, Mom, I didn't think you'd be this mad!"

It's the Thought That Counts

Firebox.com offers its shoppers an alternative to the perfectly gift-wrapped present: CrapWrap. "This uniquely shoddy option involves us wrapping your presents in a slapdash fashion," boasts the site. For $5.90, each gift is guaranteed "Too much brown tape . . . uneven edges," and "rips in the packaging exposing the surprise underneath."

➡ That Reminds Me of a Joke

"I bought my brother some gift wrap for Christmas. I took it to the gift wrap department and told them to wrap it, but in a different print so he would know when to stop unwrapping."

—Steven Wright

He Seems Nice, but You Gotta Watch Grandpa

When a seven-year-old girl called 911 and then hung up, the Burnett, Wisconsin, police were dispatched to her home. When cops arrived, they discovered the problem—the girl's grandfather was cheating in a game of cards.

Source: Ananova.com

 ## That Reminds Me of a Joke

"My grandfather always said, "Don't watch your money; watch your health." So one day while I was watching my health, someone stole my money. It was my grandfather."

—Jackie Mason

Bonus Joke

To my friend's astonishment, a police car pulled up to her house and her elderly grandfather got out. The patrolman explained that the old gentleman had been lost in the city park and had asked for help.

"Why, Grandfather," my friend said, "you've been going there for 40 years. How could you get lost?"

The old man smiled slyly. "Wasn't exactly lost," he admitted. "I just got tired of walking."

—Clara Harshfield

You Look Familiar

Los Angeles twins Becky and Amy Glass are so close, they haven't been apart for more than 30 minutes in 15 years. They also dress exactly alike every day, and they share a Facebook profile, a business, a cell phone, a bedroom, and once even a boyfriend. And to make sure that they remain looking alike, they measure all their food to ensure that they eat the same amount.

Source: web.orange.co.uk

That Reminds Me of a Joke

A woman has twins and gives them up for adoption. One of them goes to a family in Egypt and is named Amal. The other goes to a family in Spain; they name him Juan. Years later, Juan sends a picture of himself to his mother. Upon receiving the picture, she tells her husband that she wished she also had a picture of Amal.

Her husband responds, "They're twins. If you've seen Juan, you've seen Amal."

ı ı

No Way to Gitmo Action

A Saudi woman filed for divorce from her husband of 17 years after peeking through the contacts in his cell phone. Next to her phone number, she found the nickname Guantanamo.

Source: *The Telegraph* (London)

 That Reminds Me of a Joke

A guy is walking around in a supermarket yelling, "Crisco, Crisco?"

A store clerk says to him, "Sir, the Crisco is in Aisle Five."

The guys says, "I'm not looking for cooking Crisco, I'm calling my wife."

"Your wife is named 'Crisco'?"

"No, I only call her that in public."

The clerk says, "What do you call her when you're home?"

"Lard butt."

I I I I I I I I I I I I I I I I I I I I I I I I I I I I I I I I I I I I I I I I I I I I I I I

Well, She *Is* Man's Best Friend

Graham Anley was sailing from to Madagascar, when his yacht ran aground off the coast of East London, South Africa, and was severely damaged. Anley scooped up his nine-year-old Jack Russell terrier, Rosie, and swam ashore to safety. Only when he was assured that his dog would be all right did Anley swim back to the yacht to save his other traveling companion—his wife.

Source: news24.com

 That Reminds Me of a Joke

Why dogs are better than women:

Dogs don't mind if you leave the seat up; in fact, they prefer it.

Dogs don't like cats.

Dogs don't care what you say to other drivers.

▮▮▮

One Spouse Is Enough

Prior to his wedding day, a Japanese man knew there was likely one person who would probably object: the woman he was already married to. So he did what any sane man might—he set fire to the hotel where the wedding was to be held. "I thought if I set a fire I wouldn't have to go through with the wedding," he told the police. Nobody was hurt.

Source: Reuters

 ## That Reminds Me of a Joke

The vicar noticed that the bride was in great distress, so he asked her what was wrong.

"I'm afraid I won't remember what to do," she said.

"You only need to remember three things," he said. "First, the aisle, because that is what you'll be walking down. Secondly, the altar, because that is where you will arrive. And finally, remember the hymn, because that is a type of song we will sing during the service."

While the bride was walking to the wedding march, the groom was horrified to hear her repeating these three words . . . Aisle, altar, hymn, aisle, altar, hymn . . .

Do You Sell Eau de New Car Smell?

If you can't get enough of that just-left-a-bar smell, we've got the perfumery for you. Demeter Fragrance believes their scents should mirror the real world, hence their popular Gin & Tonic fragrance. Here are a few more scents their customers are splashing on:

- Hot Fudge Sundae Fragrance
- Laundromat Fragrance
- Blueberry Muffin Fragrance
- Play-Doh Fragrance

➤ That Reminds Me of a Joke

The man walked over to the perfume counter and told the clerk he would like a bottle of Christian Dior for his wife's birthday.

"A little surprise, eh?" asked the clerk.

"Yes," replied the man. "She's expecting a cruise."

The Son Never Rises

An Italian couple is trying to evict their son from their home. The reason? He's 41 years old and in no hurry to leave. "He has a good job but . . . wants his clothes washed and ironed and his meals cooked for him. He never wants to leave," the disgruntled father complained.

Source: web.orange.co.uk

 That Reminds Me of a Joke

A father is lecturing his lazy son. "All you do is sit around the house all day!"

"Well, what would I get if I had a job?" says the son.

"You'd get a salary and a pension," replies the father. "You'd be able to settle down and retire and not work anymore."

The son shrugs. "I do that now."

An Added Wrinkle

Robert Edward Tyrell, of Villa Rica, Georgia, was arrested on charges of aggravated assault and false imprisonment. The victim: His mother. What caused him to blow up: She refused to do his ironing.

Source: Orange (England) News

That Reminds Me of a Joke

"Alligators have the right idea: They eat their young."

—Ida Corwin, in Mildred Pierce

ıı

How Was His Handwriting?

For Dick Kleis, flowers and a box of chocolates won't cut it when it comes to celebrating his wife's birthday. So for Carole's 67th, he wrote a massive "HAP B DAY LUV U" in the cornfield of their Zwingle, Iowa, farm. That's not so strange, but the ink he used was: 123,850 pounds of cow dung. "I was going to put a heart there after happy birthday," he told thonline.com, "but I ran out of manure."

That Reminds Me of a Joke

A little boy runs across a farmer who has a truckload of cow manure. The boy asks him what he is going to do with the cow poop. The farmer tells the little boy, "I'm taking it home to put on my strawberries."

The little boy looks up at the farmer and says, "I don't know where you come from, but where I come from we put cream and sugar on our strawberries."

What Makes You Think He's Still Angry?

A Michigan man bought the house next door to his ex-wife and erected a giant statue of a clenched fist with one finger extended so that it faced her home. Which finger? Here's a hint: It's not the thumb, it's not the index finger, it's not the ring finger, and it's not the pinky.

Source: dailymail.co.uk

 That Reminds Me of a Joke

You know your marriage is in trouble when your wife starts wearing her wedding ring on the middle finger.

—Dennis Miller

Luckily, There Was No Mention of the Kids

At the conclusion of his divorce proceedings, a Serbian judge ordered a man to share all his property equally with his soon to be ex-wife, including his beloved farm equipment. Following the judgment to the letter, he purchased a grinder and cut all his tools and machinery in half.

Source: Reuters

That Reminds Me of a Joke

When we divorced, we shared the house 50/50. She got the inside; I got the outside.

Bonus Joke

My law partner was presenting a no-fault divorce case to an Ohio domestic-relations court. The couple involved had no children, but they did have a dog, of whom both were very fond.

My partner stated that both parties agreed to share whatever medical expenses might be necessary for the care of the animal. They also agreed that the wife would have custody, but that the husband would be allowed visitation rights.

The judge, looking somewhat startled, peered down at the husband and asked, "Is this true?"

The husband replied, "Yes, Your Honor."

"Well," intoned the judge, with a trace of a smile on his face, "you should know that there is nothing this court can do for you if the dog refuses to see you."

—Stephen G. Meckler

I Wondered Why the Dog Sent Me a Thank-You Card

Alf Spence's family had thought that he'd forgotten their birthdays because they never received a card from him. Turns out the elderly Brit did remember, only problem is, instead of depositing his cards and letters into the red bin for mail, he was depositing them into a nearby red bin for dog droppings.

Source: anorak.co.uk

 That Reminds Me of a Joke

A cop pulls over an elderly man for driving too slowly. "Officer, What's wrong? I was going the speed limit, 22 miles an hour."

"Sir, that's the route number," says the officer. Just then, he notices the driver's wife in the passenger seat. Her eyes are bulging and she's as white as a ghost. "What's wrong with her?

"Oh, she'll be all right in a minute. We just got off Route 175."

Is There an Opening on the Chain Gang?

An Italian man under house arrest for drug dealing begged authorities to show leniency and put him in jail so that he could escape his nagging wife. According to authorities, he asked police to let him serve the rest of his sentence behind bars "because living with his wife was particularly difficult and unbearable." The police were happy to oblige.

Source: thelocal.it

That Reminds Me of a Joke

After 12 years in prison, a man finally escapes. When he gets home, filthy and exhausted, his wife says, "Where have you been? You escaped eight hours ago!"

Bonus Joke

A woman is brought to court after stealing from a supermarket.

"Mrs. Krupnick," says the judge, "what did you take?"

"Just a small can of peaches," she answers. "There were only six peaches in the can."

"Six peaches . . . hmm . . . I sentence you to six nights in jail, a night for each peach."

The woman is crushed. She's about to collapse to the floor when her husband, seated in the gallery, leaps to his feet.

"Your Honor," he shouts, "she also stole a can of peas!"

Here's to You, Ms. All Things Nice

Charlotte Price of Great Britain is obsessed with the color pink. The mother of three wears pink, her house is pink, she works in a pink hair salon, and now her name is Pink. Price legally had it changed to Pink Sparkly And All Things Nice.

Source: mirror.co.uk

 That Reminds Me of a Joke

"I have a pal in England who was christened Cuthbert de la Hay Horace. Fortunately, everyone calls him Stinker."

—P. G. Wodehouse

I I I I I I I I I I I I I I I I I I I I I I I I I I I I I I I I I I I I I I I I I I I I I I I

But Sisters Share Everything

A woman in Slidell, Louisiana, was arrested on charges of Medicaid fraud after checking into a hospital under her deceased sister's name. How did anyone guess she wasn't who she said she was? She was wearing the commemorative T-shirt from her sister's funeral.

Source: fox8live.com

That Reminds Me of a Joke

I can't believe I was the victim of identity theft. But on a positive note, my credit rating went up.

▪▪

At Least the Fight Was Over Something Important

An Illinois woman was charged with domestic battery during an argument on Memorial Day. The argument centered around which sister had caught the most pieces of candy tossed during the town's holiday parade.

Source: Arlington Heights (Illinois) *Daily Herald*

 That Reminds Me of a Joke

"Never let an angry sister comb your hair."

—Patricia McCann

▪▪

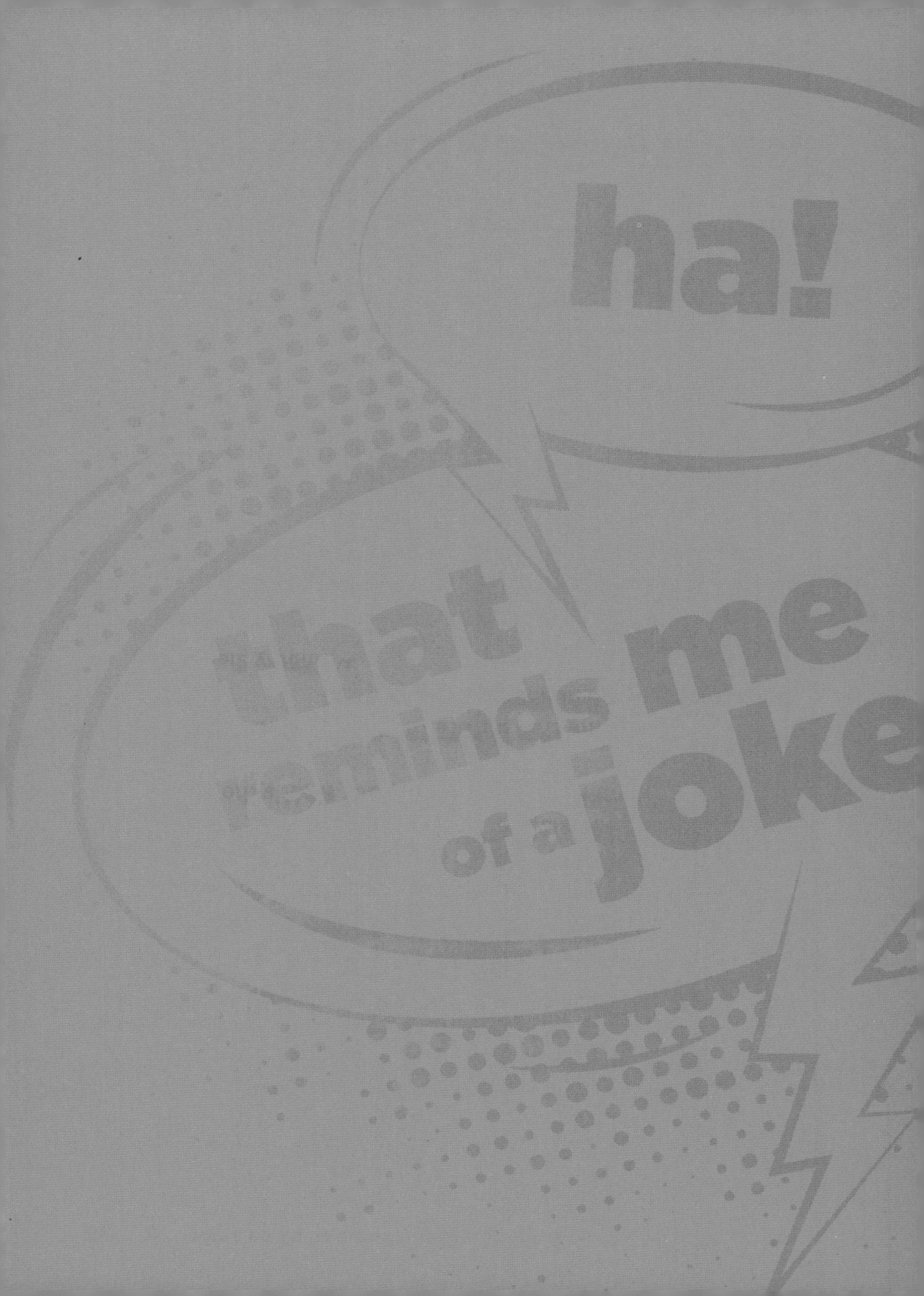
ha!
that reminds me of a joke

community
life

"Anyone who believes the competitive spirit is dead has never been in a supermarket when the cashier opens another checkout lane."

—Ann Landers

Who Gives a Dam!

When Michigan officials say, "No building without a permit," they mean it. That's what Stephen Tvedten found out when he received a letter from state officials demanding that he "cease and desist" the construction of two dams on his property.

Trouble was, it wasn't Tvedten building the dams—it was a family of beavers.

Fortunately, the state dropped its concerns once an investigator examined the situation more closely.

"It probably would have been a good idea to do the inspection before we sent the notice," one official said.

Source: snopes.com

That Reminds Me of a Joke

"The only thing that saves us from bureaucracy is its inefficiency."

—Former Senator Eugene McCarthy

▮ ▮

Living up to Its Name

In just its first month, more than a thousand people downloaded a new City Hall-approved smart-phone application for Cedar Rapids, Iowa. Residents were not deterred by its less than delicate acronym: CRapp.

Source: Cedar Rapids Gazette

 That Reminds Me of a Joke

How many bureaucrats does it take to screw in a light bulb? Seven—one to supervise, one to arrange for the electricity to be shut off, one to make sure that safety and quality standards are maintained, one to monitor compliance with local, state, and federal regulations, one to manage personnel relations, one to fill out the paperwork, and one to screw the light bulb into the water faucet.

▮ ▮

If You Disagree, Hiss

The city of Wheeling, Illinois, plans to build a $1.2 million paved bike and pedestrian path. People who use the path will most likely spend much of their time sprinting, as it happens to run adjacent to the habitat of the highly poisonous Eastern massasauga rattlesnake.

Source: stltoday.com/*St. Louis Post-Dispatch*

 ## That Reminds Me of a Joke

Two campers are in the woods when one is bitten on the butt by a snake. "I'll go into town for a doctor," the other says.

He runs 10 miles to a small town and finds the only doctor for miles helping a woman deliver a baby. "I can't leave," the doctor says. "But here's what you do. Take a knife, cut a huge X where the bite is, suck out the poison, and spit it on the ground."

The guy runs back to his friend, who is in agonizing pain. "What did the doctor say?" the victim asks.

The friend said, "He says you're going to die."

That Translates to "Ooops"

A bilingual road sign near Cardiff, Wales, caught bikers off guard. The English part read "Cyclists Dismount." The Welsh: "Llid Y Bledren Dymchwelyd," or "Bladder disease has returned." One theory for the mistake—instead of typing "cyclist" into a translation program, someone typed "cystitis."

Source:walesonline.co.uk

That Reminds Me of a Joke

A missionary goes to Africa to visit a very old, primitive tribal community. He gives a long sermon. For half an hour he tells a long anecdote, and then the interpreter stands up. He speaks only four words and everyone laughs uproariously. The missionary is puzzled. How is it possible that a story half an hour long can be translated in four words? What kind of amazing language is this? Puzzled, he says to the interpreter, "You have done a miracle. You have spoken only four words. I don't know what you said, but how can you translate my story, which was so long, into only four words?"

The interpreter says, "Story too long, so I say, 'He says joke—laugh!'"

He Only Had a Few Feet to Go

A German man was stopped by police for riding an unsafe motorcycle. "You have no brake on the right of your handlebar," the officer told Bogdan Ionescu. Ionescu had a ready excuse: He didn't have a right arm. So he had modified the bike to fit his needs. The officer, a stickler for rules, didn't care, and fined Ionescu 25 euros.

Source: thelocal.de

That Reminds Me of a Joke

Q: How do you make a one-armed biker fall off his Harley?
A: Wave.

Q: Where did the one-handed man buy his motorcycle?
A: At a secondhand bike shop.

Bonus Joke

A Harley rider eating in a restaurant is checking out a gorgeous redhead. Suddenly she sneezes, and her glass eye comes flying out of its socket. The biker reaches up, snatches it out of the air, and hands it back to her. "I am so embarrassed," the woman says. "Please join me for dinner."

They enjoy a wonderful meal together, and afterwards she invites him to the theater, followed by drinks. She pays for everything. Then she asks him to her place for a nightcap and to stay for breakfast.

The next morning the guy is amazed. "Are you this nice to every biker you meet?" he asks.

"Not usually," she replies. "But you just happened to catch my eye."

¡ ¡

Title Redacted!

Everyone's familiar with the hyper-protective school boards that ban books because of controversial language. But few can match the visionary leaders of the Menifee Union School District in California, who decided that the best way to handle certain words was to ban the dictionary.

"It's hard to sit and read the dictionary, but we'll be looking to find other things of a graphic nature," a district spokesperson said.

A district committee reversed the ban.

Source: theguardian.com

 ## That Reminds Me of a Joke

Censorship ends in logical completeness when nobody is allowed to read any books except the books that nobody reads.

—George Bernard Shaw

¡ ¡

That'll Teach You to Return the Lawn Mower Next Time

Following a dispute, a man allegedly tossed a Molotov Cocktail at his neighbor's trailer home in Bithlo, Florida . . . just as the winds shifted, sending embers on to his own trailer. Luckily for him he was sent to jail, since he no longer had a home of his own to return to.

Source: cfnews13.com

 ## That Reminds Me of a Joke

I came from a real tough neighborhood. In the local restaurant I sat down and had broken leg of lamb.

—Rodney Dangerfield

Part A Goes into Part Z which Goes into Part L which Goes into . . .

Police were called to a Swedish apartment at one in the morning after neighbors heard banging, followed by the sound of a baby screaming. When cops arrived, they did indeed discover the crying baby, as well as her parents attempting to assemble furniture from Ikea.

Source: thelocal.se

That Reminds Me of a Joke

"That is the last time I order anything online from Ikea.
I ordered a leather couch. They sent me a bull with
instruction on how to skin it."

@Tim McRaw

You Spell It the Way It's Pronounced

The Webster, Massachusetts, Chamber of Commerce has discovered that the name of the town lake has been misspelled on signs for years. The lake they incorrectly spelled Chargoggagoggmanchaoggagoggchaubuna-guhgamaugg is actually spelled Chargoggagoggmanch-auggagoggchaubunagungamaugg.

Source: *Worcester (Massachusetts) Telegram & Gazette*

 ## That Reminds Me of a Joke

Two tourists were driving through Louisiana when they noticed a sign welcoming them to Natchitoches. They wondered about the pronunciation. One thought it was pronounced NATCH-ee-toe-cheese, and the other insisting it as Natch-eye-TOTT-chez. They stopped by a burger joint and asked the woman behind the counter, "We need a local to settle an argument for us. Could you please pronounce where we are . . . very slowly."

The woman leaned over and said as distinctly as she could, "Brrrrrr, grrrrrr, Kiiiinngg."

Something Doesn't Smell Right

A retiree in Teaneck, New Jersey, was arrested for threatening his neighbor. What had the neighbor done to raise the retiree's ire? He passed gas as he walked by the retiree's door.

Source: nj.com

That Reminds Me of a Joke

Two airline mechanics get off work from Kennedy Airport and one says, "Let's go have a beer."

The other says, "Why don't we try drinking jet fuel? I hear it tastes like whiskey, without the hangover." So they drink a quart apiece.

The next morning, one of them calls up the other and says, "How do you feel?"

"Great."

"Me, too. No hangover. Just one thing, have you passed gas yet?"

"No."

"Well, don't. I'm calling from Phoenix."

⁚⁚⁚

Even Dead He's a Better Candidate

Tim Murray ran for Congress in Oklahoma this past year, trying to unseat the incumbent Frank Lucas. Murray thought he had an excellent shot at winning since Lucas was ineligible to run, he insisted. According to Murray, the person running as Frank Lucas was actually a body double since the real Frank Lucas was televised being executed by the World Court in the Ukraine earlier that year. Lucas denied having been executed and easily won reelection.

Source: KFOR

That Reminds Me of a Joke

"Politics is not a bad profession. If you succeed, there are many rewards. If you disgrace yourself, you can always write a book."

—Ronald Reagan

Bonus Joke

I looked up the word politics in the dictionary. It's actually a combination of two words: *poli,* which means many, and *tics*, which means bloodsuckers.

—Jay Leno

www.shutupalready.com

When a neighbor wanted to let an amorous couple in his apartment building know just how little privacy they had, he renamed his Wi-Fi network—which could be seen anytime anyone logged on to their own network—"We can all hear you having sex."

Source: slate.com

 ## That Reminds Me of a Joke

A salesman was given a hotel room next to one occupied by honeymooners. The walls were thin, and the sounds of love-making filtered through. Finally the salesman could stand it no longer. He pounded on the walls, yelling, "Knock it off! People are trying to sleep!"

From the other room came a weak, faltering male voice which said, "Yell louder, mister, she can't hear you!"

▪ ▪

Don't Drink the Lemonade

The new city hall in Chandler, Arizona, is eco-friendly and uses recycled gray water in the toilets. As a result, a sign went up in the bathrooms warning employees not to drink out of the toilets. "I'm glad I saw that sign because I was very thirsty," deadpanned the mayor.

Source: azcentral.com

That Reminds Me of a Joke

"I just found out why dogs drink out of the toilet. My mother said it's because the water is a lot colder in there. I'm like, How does my mother know that?"

—Wendy Liebman

▪▪

Perfect for Short Trips

In an effort to encourage green transportation, the city of Cardiff, Wales, spent $3,200 on a new bike lane, the shortest in Great Britain, possibly the world. The lane is eight feet long and takes one second to traverse before rejoining traffic.

Source: *The Telegraph* (London)

 ## That Reminds Me of a Joke

A pedestrian stepped off the curb and into the road without looking and promptly got knocked flat by a passing cyclist.

"You were really lucky there," said the cyclist.

"What are you talking about? That hurt!" said the pedestrian.

The cyclist replied, "Usually I drive a bus."

▪▪

Doing My Patriotic *HIC* Duty

Russia's former minister of finance, Alexei Kudrin, knows a way to generate taxes and goose his country's sluggish economy: Everyone should drink and smoke more.

"Those who drink, those who smoke are doing more to help the state," he said.

Source: telegraph.co.uk

That Reminds Me of a Joke

"Here's to alcohol: the cause of, and solution to, all of life's problems."

—Homer Simpson

I I I I I I I I I I I I I I I I I I I I I I I I I I I I I I I I I I I I I I I I I I I I I I

Dental Flaws

After imbibing heavily at her young son's birthday party, Tina Gonzales of Naples, Florida, got into a fight with her neighbor and ended up biting her. Cops were able to pin it on Gonzales by counting the tooth marks on the victim. That's because Gonzales was the only person present with all her teeth.

Source: *Palm Beach Sun-Sentinel*

That Reminds Me of a Joke

Do you know why it's so hard to solve a redneck murder? 'Cause there's no dental records and all the DNA is the same.

—Jeff Foxworthy

Well, La-di-da, Look at Tim Gunn Over There!

A 13-year-old student in England was punished and spent a day in educational isolation for violating the school's dress code. His crime: Forgoing a clip-on tie in favor of a regular tie.

Source: *The Telegraph* (London)

That Reminds Me of a Joke

"If men can run the world, why can't they stop wearing neckties? How intelligent is it to start the day by tying a little noose around your neck?"

—Linda Ellerbee

He Saved Money on Stamping "L"s

The head of the Chilean national mint lost his job after the country's new fifty-peso coin was released. Instead of "Republica de Chile," it read, "Republica de Chiie." Bonus stupidity: It took a year for someone to discover the mistake.

Source: BBC news

 ## That Reminds Me of a Joke

How do you spell wrong?
　　R-o-n-g.
　　That's wrong.
　　That's what you asked for, isnt it?

Bonus Joke

Our son recently married a Russian woman. During the reception, Russian and American guests proposed toasts. As someone translated, my sister-in-law said, "Good health, good fortune. Go and multiply."

　　I couldn't help noticing that some of the guests looked confused. We found out later that this had been translated as, "Good health, good fortune. Go and do math."

—David A. Macleod

Can't Blame Him, a Lot of People Have Been Trying to Forget All About Washington Lately

Justin Gray almost didn't get a chance to board his flight out of Orlando. That's because when asked for identification, he showed the TSA agent his Washington, D.C., driver's license. What was wrong with that? Nothing, except that the TSA agent insisted that the District of Columbia license was an invalid form of ID because the agent had never heard of the District of Columbia. Gray was able to convince the agent that, indeed, it was a real place, and boarded his plane.

Source: WFTV (Orlando)

That Reminds Me of a Joke

"If it weren't for being frisked at the airport, I'd have no sex life."

—Rodney Dangerfield

The True Christmas Spirit

From the Westfield (Massachusetts) Evening News Police Log: "A caller reports that her neighbors are having another argument; the responding officer reports the resident was alone and not intoxicated but was having a disagreement with his Christmas tree which was giving him trouble as he was taking it down."

That Reminds Me of a Joke

Each year, a boy asks his father to get a Christmas tree, and each year the father tells him, "I don't want to pay for it." But the son keeps begging. Unable to bear his son's whining, he picks up his axe one day and heads out of the house.

Thirty minutes later he returns with a great big Christmas tree. "How did you cut it down so fast?" his son asks.

"I didn't cut it down," the father replies. "I got it at a tree lot."

"Then why did you bring an axe?"

"Because I didn't want to pay."

▪ ▪

He's Seriously Running

The late Dr. Barry Commoner, an ecologist who ran for president in 1980, wanted to make environmental concerns an issue in the race but had little luck. "The peak of the campaign happened in Albuquerque," he later recalled. "A local reporter said to me, 'Dr. Commoner, are you a serious candidate or are you just running on the issues?'"

Source: nytimes.com

That Reminds Me of a Joke

At the turn of the century, a politician goes to an Indian reservation to try and drum up support. He stands on a barrel and delivers a rousing speech. First he promises less taxes and his audience replies by shouting, "Hoya! Hoya!"

He then promises better public facilities. "Hoya! Hoya!" shouts his audience.

The politician is delighted and then promises to increase the reservation lands by fifty percent. The crowd yells back, "Hoya! Hoya!"

"This is fantastic!" he thinks. "They're eating out of my hand." He gets off his barrel and, as the Chief escorts him out, says, "I think it went pretty well."

The chief nods his head, then says, "Hey, watch your shoes! You almost stepped in that big pile of hoya."

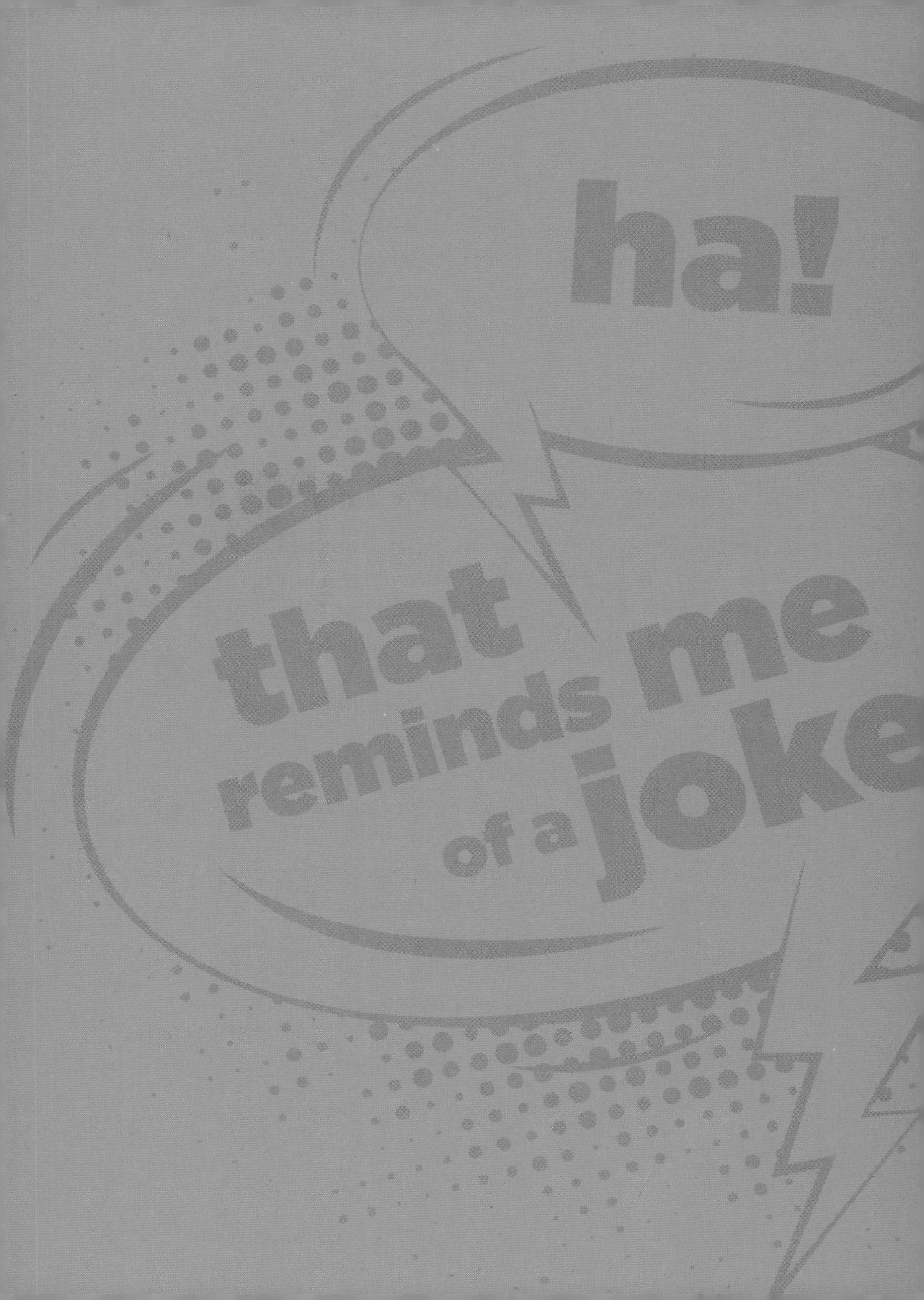
ha!
that reminds me of a joke

the digital age

"I took a two-year-old computer in to be repaired, and the guy looked at me as though he was a gun dealer and I'd brought him a musket. In two years, I'd gone from cutting-edge to Amish."

—Jon Stewart

Status Update: Embarrassed

When two Australian girls, aged 10 and 12, got stuck in a storm drain, they were lucky to have a cell phone and reception. And they quickly put that technology to work. No, they didn't call police—they updated their Facebook statuses to "Lost under the streets." The girls were eventually rescued, but only after friends called for help.

Source: switched.com

That Reminds Me of a Joke

Thank God for Facebook. Otherwise, I'd have to call 674 people everyday to tell them I went to the gym.

Source: Rottenecards.com

Bonus Joke

My neighbor, a police officer, pulled someone over for texting while driving, a big no-no in our state. The driver was having none of it.

"I was not texting!" she insisted indignantly. "I was on Facebook."

—Brenda Morales

▪▪

Of Course, Hell Has Lousy Reception

A Polish priest complained that a demon that he had tried to exorcise responded by sending him text messages over and over again. Said the priest: "The owners of mobile phones are not even aware that they're being used like this."

Source: dailymail.co.uk

 ## That Reminds Me of a Joke

What film had a minister trying to develop a cell phone application for exorcism? "The Last Apps-orcism."

▪▪

Still, His Office *Is* Beautiful

This correction ran in a recent issue of *Vogue:* "In the September profile of Chelsea Clinton, Dan Baer was mistakenly identified as an interior designer. He is a deputy assistant secretary for the Bureau of Democracy, Human Rights, and Labor at the U.S. Department of State."

Source: thewire.com

 That Reminds Me of a Joke

Deciding to take a day off from his job, a young hotshot broker went back to visit some of his professors at his old school. Entering the school, he saw a dog attacking a small child. He quickly jumped on the dog and strangled it.

The next day, the local paper reported the story with the headline "Valiant Student Saves Boy From Fearsome Dog."

The broker called the editor of the paper and strongly suggested that a correction be issued, pointing out that he was no longer a student but a successful Wall Street broker.

The following day, the paper issued a correction, with a headline that read, "Pompous Stock Broker Kills School Mascot."

․ ․

Defaced-Book

It's a mistake anyone could have made. Rather than typing "Facebook" into his Apple computer's browser, a Tennessee lawyer inadvertently typed "f***book." Shockingly, it turns out that the latter site contained pornography, which appealed to the lawyer's "biological sensibilities." Since the snafu has resulted in his becoming addicted to porn, he's suing Apple for not warning computer users against the evils of porn.

Source: pcmag.com

That Reminds Me of a Joke

The devil visited a lawyer's office and made him an offer.

"I can arrange some things for you," the devil said. "I'll increase your income five-fold. Your partners will love you; your clients will respect you; you'll have four months of vacation each year and live to be a hundred. All I require in return is your wife's soul, your children's souls, and their children's souls for eternity."

The lawyer thought for a moment, then asked, "Okay, what's the catch?"

I I I I I I I I I I I I I I I I I I I I I I I I I I I I I I I I I I I I I I I I I I I I I I I I I

Calling Walter Cronkite

An Atlanta news anchor led off the program with this breaking story: "A pond the size of a football field is on fire at a prison in Jackson County. It is a detention pond." After a quick reread, she made this edit: "It is a retention pond."

On a story about safe driving, a BBC anchorwoman made this cunning observation: "Most cars on our roads have only one occupant, usually the driver."

From the department of the stunningly obvious comes this statement from a reporter at the scene of a murder: "Some people in this neighborhood feel this should never have happened."

That Reminds Me of a Joke

The local TV anchorman announces, "Two Brazilian men died in a skydiving accident."

His co-anchor shakes her head and says, "That's horrible. So many men dying that way."

▪▪▪

Spamalot

Spammers may not be the most respectable of entrepreneurs. But they give it their best shot when it comes to the names they give the purported email senders:

- Spurious Ponder
- Elfleda Yates
- Piety Cutler
- Miroslawa Lovelace
- Pericles Childs
- Sylvain Motley
- Clotilda Starks
- Booth Julio

From utterzebo.com

 That Reminds Me of a Joke

If life were structured like email, most of my friends would be sent to the Spam folder.

—Jane Bot

I Like Quiet When I Eat My Bagel

Editors at the *New York Times* were forced to run this correction: "A column earlier this month about introverts and extroverts misquoted the French Philosopher Jean-Paul Sartre. The correct quote is 'Hell is other people,' not 'Hell is other people at breakfast.'"

Source: poynter.org

That Reminds Me of a Joke

Jean-Paul Sartre is sitting at a French cafe, revising his draft of *Being and Nothingness.* He says to the waitress, "I'd like a cup of coffee, please, with no cream."

The waitress replies, "I'm sorry, Monsieur, but we're out of cream. How about with no milk?"

▌▌▌

Wake Me When It's Recess

South Bend, Indiana's WNDU-TV news crew was worried that local schools were letting students coast through classes. In response, the news show produced a segment on the topic, one possibly scripted by a graduate of said school district. The title of the report: "School Two Easy For Kids."

Source: Gawker.com

➡️ That Reminds Me of a Joke

Did you hear about the kid whose teacher told him to write a 100-word essay on what he did on vacation? He wrote "Not much" 50 times.

Bum Rap

The scientific community has bestowed one of its highest honors on the singer Beyoncé: It named an insect after her. A newly discovered horsefly will now be known as Scaptia (Plinthina) beyonceae. The reason she was so honored: Both, it appears, share prominent backsides.

Source: earthsky.org

That Reminds Me of a Joke

Beyoncé's booty is so big, by the time she put on her BVDs, they spelled "boulevard."

··

Blonde Ambition

During the past year's Miss USA pageant, Miss Ohio was asked whether or not movies and TV depict women in an accurate and positive light. Her response: Yes. The film she used to bolster her argument? *Pretty Woman,* the Julia Roberts film about a prostitute. Maybe this explains why she came in second.

Source: thehollywoodgossip.com

➡ That Reminds Me of a Joke

A beauty pageant contestant wanted to buy personalized license plates but she couldn't afford them. So she changed her name to DBT432.

Bonus Joke

At a convention of blondes, a speaker insisted that the "dumb blonde" myth is all wrong. To prove it he asked one cute young volunteer, "How much is 101 plus 20?"

The blonde answered, "120."

"No," he said, "that's not right."

The audience called out, "Give her another chance."

So the speaker asked the blonde, "How much is 10 plus 13?"

Slowly the blonde replied, "16."

"Sorry," he said, shaking his head.

Once again the crowd roared, "Give her another chance."

"This is your last try," warned the speaker. "How much is 2 plus 2?"

Carefully she ventured, "Four?"

And the crowd yelled, "Give her another chance!"

—James T. Dorsey

Hold the Presses!

Actual headlines from newspapers:

"Worker suffers leg pain after crane drops 800-pound ball on his head."

"City unsure why the sewer smells."

"Caskets found as workers demolish mausoleum."

"Statistics show that teen pregnancy drops off significantly after age 25."

"Barbershop singers bring joy to school for the deaf."

"Homicide victims rarely talk to police."

"Man with 8 DUIs blames drinking problem."

"Hospitals resort to hiring doctors."

 ## That Reminds Me of a Joke

A vertically challenged psychic was arrested one day. He escaped from jail and the newspaper headline read, "SMALL MEDIUM AT LARGE."

I I I I I I I I I I I I I I I I I I I I I I I I I I I I I I I I I I I I I I I I I I I I I I I

Everybody's a Critic: Part 1

It was moving day at the Courtney Love household, and after the movers loaded the boxes and furniture onto the truck, they tossed out the garbage, including a dead bird stuffed inside a matchbox. Big mistake. It was a piece of art that the rock star had bought for $13,000.

Source: The *Daily Mail*

➡ That Reminds Me of a Joke

With his wife away, a man decided this is the perfect time to paint the toilet seat. The wife comes home sooner than expected, however, sits on the john, and the seat sticks to her rear. Panicking, she has her husband drive her to the doctor. She puts on a large overcoat so as to cover the stuck seat, and they go.

When they get to the doctor's, the husband lifts his wife's coat to show the doctor. "Have you ever seen anything like this before?" he asks.

"Well, yes," says the doctor. "But not framed."

I I I I I I I I I I I I I I I I I I I I I I I I I I I I I I I I I I I I I I I I I I I I I I I

Break a Leg

To portray drunks, German actors sipped vodka on stage. It worked, said a spectator: "They [gave] a good impersonation of tipsiness." Yes, it was theater magic—one actor stumbled off the stage and another off a table, forcing the crew to bring down the curtain early and call an ambulance.

Source: *The Telegraph* (London)

 That Reminds Me of a Joke

"You're not drunk if you can lie on the floor without holding on."

—Joe E. Lewis

No Fair, She Ordered Off the Menu!

Good Idea: How did the Tampa Woman's Club get people excited to participate in a charity? By throwing an event with plenty of champagne and giving away a $5,000 diamond. And if that weren't fun enough, the lucky winner would find the shiny bauble in her flute of bubbly!

Too bad it didn't work: When the lucky winner drank her flute of bubbly, she swallowed her shiny bauble.

Source: thedenverchannel.com

That Reminds Me of a Joke

Panicking when her toddler swallowed a tiny magnet, the mother rushed him to the emergency room.

"He'll be fine," the doctor promised her. "The magnet should pass through his system in a day or two."

"How will I be sure?" the mother asked.

"Stick him on the refrigerator. When he falls off, you'll know."

Crimea River

Have you ever wanted to be involved in an armed conflict but just didn't have the time? Good news! A sightseeing group has offered a tour of war-torn Ukraine for as little as $80. For an additional $600, visitors could watch actual combat. Best of all, according to the *Daily Mail,* some tours "include an armed guard."

Some?

That Reminds Me of a Joke

As a Russian prepares to cross the Ukrainian border, the border guard asks, "Occupation?"

"No," says the Russian. "Just visiting."

Bonus Joke

One of my jobs in the army is to give service members and their families tours of the demilitarized zone in South Korea. Before taking people to a lookout point to view North Korea, we warn visitors to watch their heads climbing the stairs, as there is a low overhang. The tour guide, first to the top, gets to see how many people have not heeded his advice.

On one tour I watched almost an entire unit hit their heads one after another as they came up the stairs. Curious, I asked their commander what unit they were from.

"Military intelligence," he replied.

—Edward Ramirez

They Went Thataway

The Coffin—a Norwegian "feel good" reality TV show about death—follows celebrities as they plan their own funerals for a TV audience. The catch: There's nothing wrong with these people . . . physically, anyway. Each show ends with the celebrity watching their casket being cremated.

Source: web.orange.co.uk

 That Reminds Me of a Joke

"They say such nice things about people at their funerals that it makes me sad that I'm going to miss mine by just a few days."

—Garrison Keillor

ı ı

Everybody's a Critic: Part 2

Worst Day on the Job: The band Kings of Leon cut short a concert after roosting pigeons bombarded them with poop. Bass player Jared Followill couldn't say how many pigeons were responsible. "The last thing I was going to do was look up," he told CNN.

 That Reminds Me of a Joke

Two blondes are walking along the beach when a seagull comes along and poops right on the head of one of them.

"Oh, no," she says. "I have bird poop on my head."

"Don't worry," says her friend. "I'll get a tissue . . . be right back!"

"Don't bother," she says. "He'll be miles away by then."

Most Honest Job Description *Ever*

Posted by the Illinois *Valley News:* "How bad do you want to be a reporter? Bad enough to work nights and weekends? In exchange for your long hours and tireless efforts you will be rewarded with low pay and marginal health insurance."

Source: journalismjobs.com

That Reminds Me of a Joke

These actual quotes—spotted on overheardinthenewsroom. com—prove that being a journalist is a tough gig.

- Editor to reporter writing about political trend story: "We better move it today. It might not be true tomorrow."

- City editor assuring a reporter: "It might get you arrested, but it won't get you fired."

- Metro editor, on story about parade floats made out of newspapers: "Can't do that with the Internet."

Where They Meet Is Much Warmer

A photo in the Brigham Young University student newspaper showed the governing body of the Mormon Church. The intended caption was, "Quorum of the Twelve Apostles," and not the one that actually ran, "Quorum of the Twelve Apostates."

Source: Associated Press

 ## That Reminds Me of a Joke

What were the last words spoken at the Last Supper?

"Everyone who wants to be in the picture, get on this side."

▮ ▮

Duck!

From The Birmingham (Alabama) News: "Corrections & Clarifications: A recipe for Italian Breaded Chicken Parmesan on Page 2G of Wednesday's Food section suggested beating the chicken with a small mallard. That, of course, is incorrect. A mallet would be a better choice."

That Reminds Me of a Joke

Doctors bury their mistakes. Lawyers hang them. But journalists put theirs on the first page.

Bonus Joke

I was editing classified ads for a small-town newspaper when a man called to place an ad. "It should read," he said, "'Free to good home. Golden retriever. Will eat anything, loves children.'"

—Ellen Young

▮ ▮

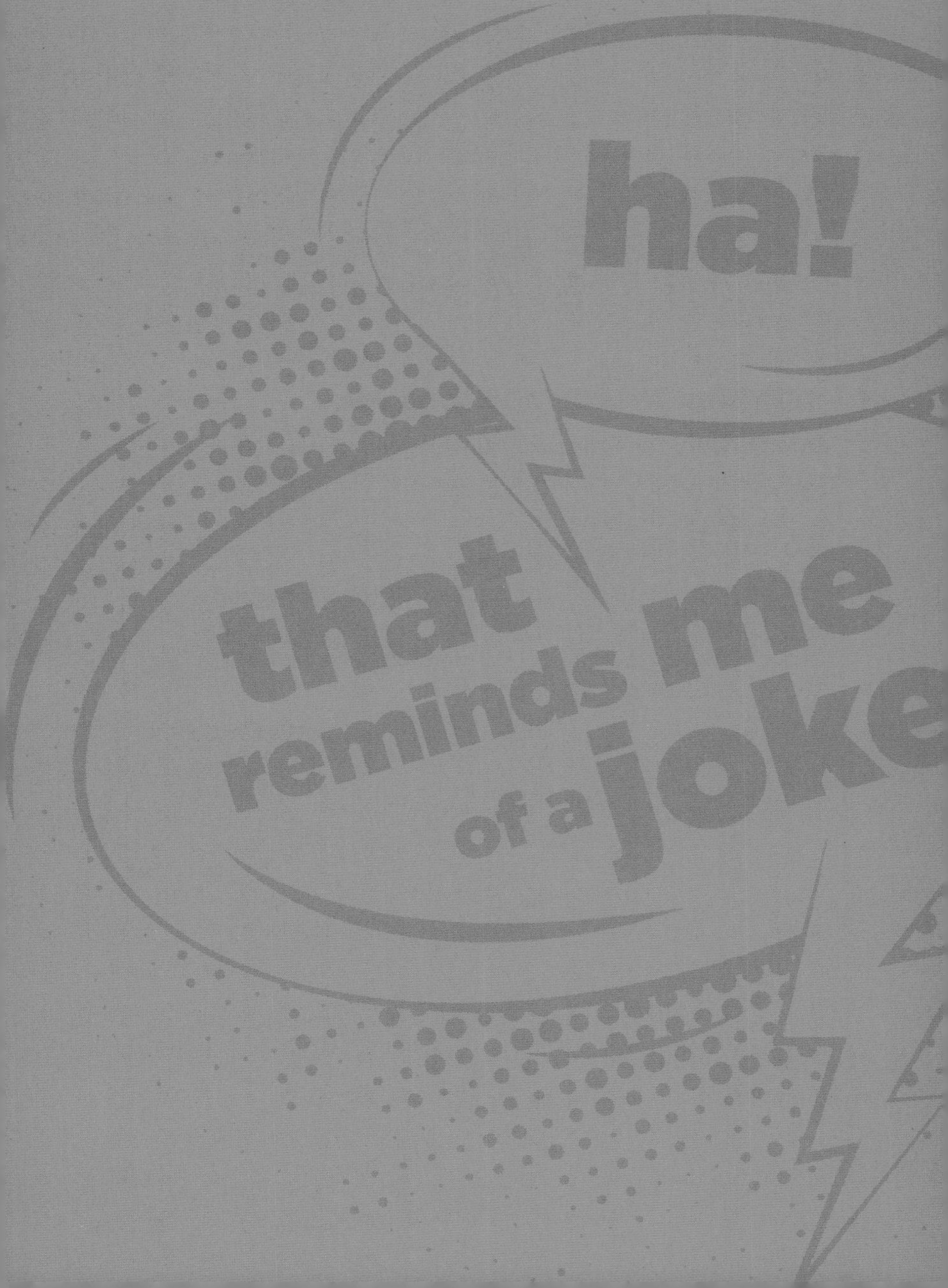
ha!
that reminds me of a joke

leisure
time

"The trouble with jogging is that
the ice falls out of your glass."

—Martin Mull

Happy Birthday, from Everyone in Town

It was a great idea: A German girl posted an invitation to her 16th birthday party on her Facebook account. Unfortunately, she neglected to mark it private. The girl canceled the party after 15,000 strangers RSVP'd. Still, 1,500 showed up at her home and partied until cops broke it up at two in the morning.

Source: thelocal.de

That Reminds Me of a Joke

A guy went to a costume party with nothing but a girl on his back.

"So what are you supposed to be?" the host asked.

"I'm a snail," the bloke replied.

"How can you be a snail when all you've got is that girl on your back?" asked the host.

"That's not a girl, that's Michelle."

Bonus Joke

As a promotional gimmick for my restaurant, I send out coupons offering people a free dinner on their birthdays. One day an anxious-sounding man called. "I got your card. How did you find me?"

"From a mailing list I purchased from a supplier," I told him. "Why?"

"It used my real name, and I'm in the Witness Protection Program. What's the name of the company?"

I didn't want to say it, but I had to tell him the truth: Moving Targets.

—Roy Harrington

Book Your Holiday Vacation Early!

From a travel article on the Woolacombe Bay Hotel in Devon: "Their three-night half-board Christmas break includes a packed program of family entertainment, a crèche, excellent cuisine, and a visit from Satan."

 **That Reminds Me of a Joke**

On Christmas Eve, everyone in town goes to their local church. Suddenly, at the altar, Satan appears! Everyone starts screaming and running for the front entrance, trampling each other to get away from Evil Incarnate. Soon, everyone is evacuated from the church except for one man, who sits calmly in his pew.

Satan walks up to the man and says, "Hey, don't you know who I am?"

The man says, "Yep, sure do."

"Well, aren't you afraid of me?"

"Nope, sure ain't."

Satan, perturbed, says, "And why aren't you afraid of me?"

The man says, "Well, I've been married to your sister for 25 years."

▪ ▪

Everything Else Sort of Works

The captain of a Vueling Airlines flight in Madrid, Spain, greeted passengers with this announcement: "We have a safety problem with the door at the front. Don't worry, it's only a safety problem."

From *The Titanic Awards*
by Doug Lansky

➡ That Reminds Me of a Joke

A doctor, a lawyer, a little boy, and a priest were flying on a small private plane. Suddenly, the plane developed engine trouble and started to go down. The pilot grabbed a parachute, yelled to the passengers that they had better jump, and bailed out. Unfortunately, there were only three parachutes remaining.

The doctor grabbed one and said, "I'm a doctor, I save lives, so I must live," and jumped out.

The lawyer said, "I'm a lawyer and lawyers are the smartest people in the world. I deserve to live." He also grabbed a parachute and jumped.

The priest said to the little boy, "My son, I've lived a long and full life. You are young and have your whole life ahead of you. Take the last parachute and live in peace."

The little boy handed the parachute back to the priest and said, "Not to worry, Father. The smartest man in the world just took off with my backpack."

Luckily, He Wasn't Awake to See the Call

When a Belgian soccer player fell to the ground after a hit from an opponent, he was promptly booted out of the game for pretending to be hurt (aka flopping), a big no-no in the sport. But the only way the player could leave the field was via a cart. That's because he'd been knocked unconscious.

Source: *Sports Illustrated*

 That Reminds Me of a Joke

If God wanted man to play soccer, he wouldn't have given us arms.

—Mike Ditka

· ·

After That, the Passengers Cleaned the Plane and Lost the Luggage

After one of its planes broke down shortly after landing, Shandong Airlines asked the passengers to push it half a mile to the gate. "Thank God it was only a 20-ton medium-sized plane," said an airport worker.

From *The Titanic Awards*
by Doug Lansky

That Reminds Me of a Joke

You know you are on a budget airline when:

- You can't board the plane unless you have the exact change.

- Before you take off, the flight attendant tells you to fasten your Velcro.

- The pilot asks all the passengers to chip in a little for fuel.

Bonus Joke

I have a cousin who was on a plane that had taken off and was approaching cruising altitude when one of the flight attendants came on the public-address system. She announced that she was sorry, but the plane's restroom was out of order. The flight attendant went on to apologize to the passengers for any inconvenience.

But then she finished cheerily with: "So, as compensation, free drinks will be served."

—Manjiri V. Oak

A Fish Tale

A British fisherman won a trophy and $1,300 when he landed the largest bass during a fishing tournament. He was later arrested and disqualified when it was learned that the winning fish had been stolen from an aquarium.

Source: *The Week*

➤ That Reminds Me of a Joke

A small town doctor was famous in the area for always catching large fish. One day while he was on one of his frequent fishing trips he got a call that a woman at a neighboring farm was giving birth. He rushed to her aid and delivered a healthy baby boy. The farmer had nothing to weigh the baby with so the doctor used his fishing scales. The baby weighed 31 pounds, 13 ounces.

Bonus Joke

A guy I know was towing his boat home from a fishing trip to Lake Huron when his car broke down. He didn't have his cell phone with him, but he thought maybe he might be able to raise someone on his marine radio to call for roadside assistance.

He climbed into his boat, clicked on the radio and said, "Mayday, Mayday."

A Coast Guard officer came on and said, "State your location."

"I-75, two miles south of Standish."

After a very long pause, the officer asked, "How fast were you going when you reached shore?"

—Mary Marineau

Obviously Not a Belieber

Igor Vorozhbitsyn was headed toward his favorite Russian fishing hole when he was thumped by something large, scary, and furry—a brown bear. The massive animal clawed and mauled the man, and nearly killed him. But then Vorozhbitsyn's cell phone rang, playing Justin Bieber's hit "Baby." The bear stopped his attack, listened, and immediately fled.

Source: *International Business Times*

That Reminds Me of a Joke

I owe my life to Justin Bieber. I was in a coma for two years, until a nurse played one of his songs on the radio in my room, and I had to wake up and turn it off.

Source: ribald.net

. . . .

Bad Sports

A fan of Britain's Manchester United soccer team was so irate about a referee's call that he phoned Britain's equivalent of 911 and demanded that the ref be arrested for his criminally poor judgment. In the end, however, the caller was arrested for *his* criminally poor judgment.

Source: metro.co.uk

That Reminds Me of a Joke

My girlfriend just split up with me because she thinks I'm obsessed with soccer.

I'm very upset about it; we'd been going out for three seasons.

. . . .

Isle Be Back

Being short on navigational expertise or equipment did not deter a British man from circumnavigating Great Britain. But his inadequacy as a sailor did. Keeping the coastline to his right, he spent all his fuel mistakenly circling over and over again the Isle of Sheppey, just east of London.

Source: BBC News

That Reminds Me of a Joke

The sailing party was hopelessly lost on the ocean. The sun was going down and the waves were starting to build when one of the sailors growled, "I thought you said you were the best captain in England."

"I am," replied the captain firmly, "but I'm pretty sure we're in Norway by now."

. . . .

Knit One, Purl Two, Leg Cramp Three

This is how dull marathon running is: David Babcock, a 41-year-old graphic design professor at the University of Central Michigan, thought he could make it more interesting by knitting while he ran. In doing so, he set a world record by knitting a 12-foot-long scarf while running (others have done this?!) in last year's Kansas City Marathon.

Source: kansascity.com

That Reminds Me of a Joke

A state trooper pulls alongside a speeding car. Glancing at the car, he's astonished to see that the woman behind the wheel is knitting. Realizing that she's oblivious to his flashing lights and siren, the cop rolls down his window and shouts, "PULL OVER!"

The woman rolls down her window and yells back, "NO, SCARF!"

He Heard the Important News

Detroit native Robert Schiller on calling his brother after winning the Nobel Prize in economics the day after the second game of the American League playoffs: "And I said, 'Did you hear the news?' And he said, 'The Tigers lost.'"

 ## That Reminds Me of a Joke

During the playoffs, a Tigers fan sitting in the nosebleed section spots an empty seat behind the dugout. Thinking to himself "what a waste," he makes his way down to the empty seat. When he arrives at the seat, he asks the man sitting next to it, "Is this seat taken?"

The man replies, "This was my wife's seat. She passed away. We went to every game—she was a big Tigers fan."

"I'm so sorry to hear of your loss," says the other man. "May I ask why you didn't give the ticket to a friend or a relative?"

The man replies, "They're all at the funeral."

I I I I I I I I I I I I I I I I I I I I I I I I I I I I I I I I I I I I I I I I I I I I I

Clueless

German police chastised a woman after she called their equivalent of 911 for help with a crossword puzzle clue. The Ananova news site quotes Petra Hirsch's explanation: "The clue was for the full name of a police border protection unit, so I thought they would not mind helping—but they were really rude."

 ## That Reminds Me of a Joke

What happened when the crossword champion died? They buried her six down and eight across.

▪▪

Honestly, How Many Letters Does He Really Need

In order to honor their all-star shortstop, the Colorado Rockies had planned to give away 15,000 Troy Tulowitzki collectible player jerseys to fans. Instead, they decided to honor him by misspelling his name—15,000 "Troy *Tulowizki*" jerseys were handed out to mostly oblivious fans. Said one man: "Is there something wrong with it? I hadn't noticed with the name being so long."

Source: espn.go.com

That Reminds Me of a Joke

After trick-or-treating, a teen takes a shortcut home through the cemetery. Halfway across, he's startled by a tapping noise coming from the misty shadows. Trembling with fear, he spots an old man with a hammer and chisel, chipping away at a headstone.

"I thought you were a ghost," says the relieved teen. "What are you doing working so late?"

"Oh, those idiots," grumbles the old man. "They misspelled my name!"

Great, We'll Celebrate in the Parking Lot

From a Royal Leamington (England) Spa newspaper: "The Crown Inn. Why not celebrate Christmas with us? Open every day except Christmas and Boxing Day."

 ## That Reminds Me of a Joke

Hotel porter, to guest: I hope you have a good memory for faces.

Guest: Yes. Why?

Porter: There's no mirror in the bathroom.

Bonus Joke

Our first day at a resort my wife and I decided to hit the beach. When I went back to our room to get something to drink, one of the hotel maids was making our bed. I grabbed my cooler and was on my way out when I paused and asked, "Can we drink beer on the beach?"

"Sure," she said, "but I have to finish the rest of the rooms first."

—Louis Allard

Waiter, There's a Hair in My Soup . . . Lots of Them

This'll teach Jason Pickar to grow a goatee next time. Last season, the comedian bet a friend that his beloved Redskins would beat the Philadelphia Eagles in the opening game. At stake: Pickar agreed to eat his own full beard if the Redskins lost. Well, the Redskins lost. In between bites, Pickar managed a great moment in understatement when he said, "It is really not very pleasant to eat one's own beard."

Source: Washingtonpost.com

 ## That Reminds Me of a Joke

A first grade teacher explains to her class that she is a football fan. She asks her students to raise their hands if they were football fans, too. Wanting to get on her good side, all the students raise their hands, except for one.

"Why didn't you raise your hand?" the teacher asks a little girl.

"Because I'm not a football fan. I like basketball," said the girl.

"Why?"

"Well, my parents love basketball, so I do, too.

"That's no reason. What if your parents were morons? What would you be then?"

"Then," says the girl, "I'd be a football fan."

Some Things Are Just That Important

Flames engulfing his Georgia home didn't stop Walter Serpit from doing the right thing. The disabled man ran into his burning home to save his loved one: a case of Bud Light.

 That Reminds Me of a Joke

"All right, brain. You don't like me and I don't like you, but let's just do this and I can get back to killing you with beer."

—Homer Simpson

■ ■

The Sound of Silence

A Swedish sailor radioed for help, saying that his wife had fallen overboard and drowned. When rescuers reached him, they discovered that the man was drunk. Upon further investigation, it was determined that his wife hadn't drowned or fallen off the boat. In fact, she was never *on* the boat. He'd forgotten that she was home watching TV.

Source: web.orange.co.uk

That Reminds Me of a Joke

A state trooper pulled over a driver and asked, "Sir, do you realize your wife fell out of the car several miles back?"

The driver replied, "Thank God, I thought I'd gone deaf!"

Bonus Joke

Heavy snow had buried my van in our driveway. My husband, Scott, dug around the wheels, rocked the van back and forth and finally pushed me free. I was on the road when I heard an odd noise. I got on my cell and called home.

"Thank God you answered," I said when Scott picked up. "There's this alarming sound coming under the van. For a moment I thought I was dragging you down the highway."

"And you didn't stop?"

—Paige Fairfield

' '

And We'll Throw in a Cleat

A player from the Fort Lauderdale Strikers, of the North American Soccer League, was sent to the San Antonio Scorpions in exchange for two nights of hotel lodging for the team.

Source: *Sports Illustrated*

 That Reminds Me of a Joke

Sally was driving home in Northern Arizona when she saw an elderly Navajo woman walking on the side of the road. She stopped the car and offered the woman a lift.

With a silent nod of thanks, the woman got into the car.

Resuming the journey, Sally tried to make small talk. The old woman just sat silently, until she noticed a brown bag on the seat next to Sally.

"What in bag?" she asked.

"It's a bottle of wine," said Sally. "I got it for my husband."

Speaking with the quiet wisdom of an elder, the Navajo woman said: "Good trade."

. . . .

Keeping a Stiff Upper Lip

Are you the sort of card player whose face gives it away when you get a Royal Flush? Good news! A New York City plastic surgeon has introduced "Pokertox," a program of Botox and facial fillers designed to enhance a player's "poker face."

Source: Huffingtonpost.com

That Reminds Me of a Joke

"Decided that the one phrase I do not want in my obituary is, 'Died before his Botox doctor could revive him.'"

—Conan O'Brien

▪ ▪

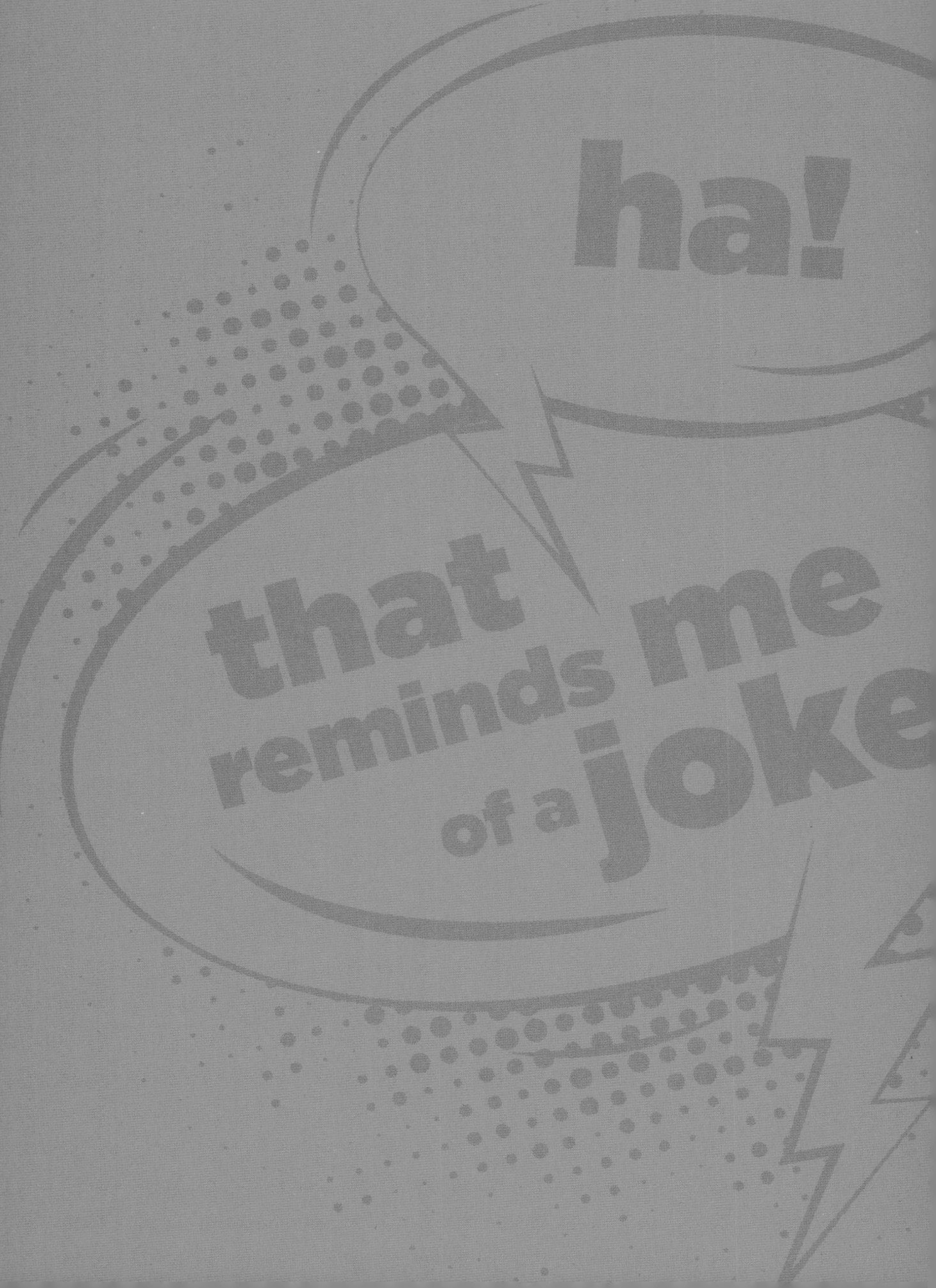
ha!
that reminds me of a joke

the daily
grind

"A professional is one who does his best work when he feels the least like working."

—Frank Lloyd Wright

He Took the Word "Break" Literally

Who hasn't experienced the feeling of helplessness after slipping a dollar bill into a vending machine only to watch the object of your desire get stuck on the coils? That's what happened to an Iowa man. But unlike the rest of us, he had a forklift at his disposal. He drove his forklift over to the recalcitrant machine and jostled it until it freed his Twix bar. Rich in chocolate, he was soon poor in employment when his boss sacked him.

Source: *The Des Moines Register*

That Reminds Me of a Joke

I like vending machines, because snacks are better when they fall.

—Mitch Hedberg

Bonus Gag:

A blonde is standing at a vending machine putting money in the slot and collecting can after can after can of Coke. A guy behind her yells, "C'mon, hurry up!"

The blonde angrily turns around and says, "Hey, can't you see I'm winning?"

It's a Miracle, I Tell Ya!

When ripping someone off, it's often best to keep a low profile. A North Carolina woman began earning workman's comp after claiming to have been so severly injured on the job that she was no longer able to lift her arms to load her mail truck. Recently, investigators grew suspicious of her claim. What tipped them off? Her limber spinning of "The Big Wheel" on the nationally syndicated game show *The Price is Right.*

Source: *New York Daily News*

That Reminds Me of a Joke

Three guys are fishing on a lake when an angel appears in the boat with them. The first guy humbly says to the angel, "I've suffered from back pain for years. Can you help me?" The angel touches the man's back, and he feels instant relief.

The second guy points to his Coke-bottle glasses and asks if the angel could cure his poor eyesight. The angel tosses the man's glasses into the lake. When they hit the water, he has 20/20 vision!

The angel now turns to the third guy, who throws up his hands in fear. "Don't touch me!" he cries. "I'm on disability!"

Who Was the Retiree, Bill Gates?

A German banker fell asleep on his keyboard halfway through a transaction. Instead of transferring 62.40 euros from a retiree's account, he deducted 222,222,222.22 euros, or the equivalent of $311 million.

Source: abc.net.au

That Reminds Me of a Joke

An accountant is having a hard time sleeping and goes to see his doctor.

"Doctor, I just can't get to sleep at night," he says.

"Have you tried counting sheep?" asks the doctor.

"That's the problem. I make a mistake and then spend three hours trying to find it."

Best Reason to Strike

Workers at the Carlsberg brewery in Denmark walked off the job after losing a prized perk: unlimited brewskies at work. Now they're limited to three at lunch. One worker told the *Wall Street Journal* that wasn't enough: "I need a beer when I take a cigarette break."

 ## That Reminds Me of a Joke

"I like beer. On occasion, I will even drink beer to celebrate a major event such as the fall of communism or the fact that the refrigerator is still working."

—Dave Barry

A Heavenly Parmigiana

Chef Jermarcus Brady found God. Literally. He was in the kitchen of Gino's Italian Restaurant in Baton Rouge when he sliced open an eggplant. Inside, the seeds were arranged in such a way that they spelled "G-O-D." This was not one of those "Does my cheeseburger look like Jesus?" type of thing. The seeds clearly read "God."

"I don't know what it means," says Brady. "All I know is it tells me 'Hey, he's real.'"

Source: WAFB.com (Baton Rouge)

That Reminds Me of a Joke

One day, a preacher who couldn't swim fell in the ocean. A boat quickly came by. "Do you need help, sir?" yelled the captain.

The preacher calmly said, "No, God will save me."

A little later, another boat came by and a fisherman asked, "Hey, do you need help?"

The preacher replied again, "No, God will save me."

Eventually the preacher drowned and went to heaven. The preacher asked God, "I don't understand. I've been a believer all my life and I've followed the principles of the Bible every day. Why didn't you save me?"

God replied, "Fool, I sent you two boats!"

Guess How Many Stupid Questions I'm Going to Ask

The big day is finally here. Your talking points are ready. Your resume is airtight. Your best suit is back from the cleaners, and you feel ready for anything . . . except, that is, when the interviewer says to you, "What's your favorite song? Perform it for us. Now." Here are other crazy questions that have been asked at job interviews:

"A penguin walks through that door wearing a sombrero. What does he say and why is he here?"

"How many windows are in New York?"

"How would you get an elephant into a refrigerator?"

That Reminds Me of a Joke

The navy psychiatrist was interviewing a potential sailor. To check on the young man's response to trouble, the psychiatrist asked, "What would you do if you looked out of that window right now and saw a battleship coming down the street?"

The sailor said, "I'd fire a torpedo and sink it."

"Where would you get the torpedo?"

"The same place you got your battleship!"

▪ ▪

Siri, for One, Is Disgusted

Imagine being the insurance rep who handled this claim: A farmer was using the light on his iPhone while assisting a cow during calving. One thing led to another, and the phone disappeared inside the back end of the cows. The phone later made an appearance, but was damaged.

Source: dailymail.co.uk

➤ That Reminds Me of a Joke

A farmer was helping a cow give birth when he noticed his four-year-old son standing wide-eyed by the fence, soaking in the whole event. After everything was over, the man, realizing this might be a teaching moment about the birds and the bees, asked his son if he had any questions.

"Just one," gasped the still wide-eyed boy. "How fast was that calf going when he hit that cow?"

▪ ▪

Sorry, That's Our Policy

How much is your tongue worth to you? If you're Gennaro Pelliccia, an Italian coffee taster, the sum is $13.9 million. That's the insurance policy he took out with Lloyd's of London. Here are some other insured body parts:

- Dolly Parton's breasts—$600,000
- Tom Jones's chest hairs—$7 million
- Michael Flatley's (Riverdance) feet—$39 million
- Egon Ronay's (food critic) taste buds—$400,000
- Ilja Gort's (winemaker) nose—$8 million
- Heidi Klum's right leg—$1.2 million
- Heidi Klum's left leg—$1 million (a scar devalues it)

➤ That Reminds Me of a Joke

Q: Why does Dolly have small feet?
A: Everything grows smaller in the shade.

Bonus Gag:

A guy goes to the doctor: "Doc, I can't stop singing 'The green, green grass of home.'"

"That sounds like Tom Jones syndrome."

"Is it common?"

"It's not unusual."

I'm Too Busy Watching Grumpy Cat

"Bob" was considered a star at the computer company where he worked. He made a six-figure salary and routinely received excellent performance reviews. And now we know why. Without his boss's knowledge, "Bob" had outsourced his entire job to a company in China—for a fifth of his salary. He then spent his days at his desk playing games, shopping on eBay, and watching cat videos.

Source: nydailynews.com

 That Reminds Me of a Joke

"I like the word *indolence.* It makes my laziness seem classy."

—Bern Williams

She's Looking for a Purrr-fectly Nice Time

This help wanted ad was spotted on Craig's List: "Feline Lap Surrogate: I work from home and I need someone to sit next to me and allow my cat to sit on their lap (the cat is attention-seeking, and has been decreasing my productivity as of late). This is a morning shift from 8am-12pm at $15/hr. I do not need anyone in the afternoon since the sun warms the windowsill by that point, and the cat will prefer the windowsill to a lap."

That Reminds Me of a Joke

"I rarely meddled in the cat's personal affairs and she rarely meddled in mine. Neither of us was foolish enough to attribute human emotions to our pets."

—Kinky Friedman

Sweet and Sour

A candy company's sales team was promised a free trip to sunny Hawaii this winter if they met their sales quota. They missed their mark, so instead got the consolation prize: a vacation in Fargo, North Dakota, where the temperature was seven degrees.

Source: Associated Press

➡ That Reminds Me of a Joke

It's January, and two candy salesmen and their boss are trying to sell chocolate bars in Alaska. They're walking along a frozen beach when they stumble upon a lamp. As they rub the lamp a genie appears and says, "Normally I would grant you three wishes, but since there are three of you, I will grant you each one wish."

The first candy salesman, wrapped in two parkas, says, "I would like to spend the rest of my life living in a hut on St. Thomas." The genie granted him his wish and sent him off to St. Thomas.

The next candy salesman moves his scarf away from his mouth just long enough to say, "I'd like to spend the rest of my life living on a huge yacht cruising the Mediterranean." The genie granted him his wish and sent him off to the Mediterranean.

The genie turned to the boss, asking, "And what would your wish be?"

"I want them both back after lunch," replied the boss. "We still have candy to sell!"

The Lazy Have Rights Too, You Know

This help-wanted ad was rejected by a British job center. Can you spot the problem?

"Domestic cleaner required immediately for local hospital. Must be fluent in written and spoken English for Health & Safety reasons. Previous experience preferred. Must be reliable and hard-working."

Give up? The offending line was the last: "Must be reliable and hard-working." The reason, as explained to Nicole Mamo, who runs the recruiting agency that posted the ad: "They could be sued for discriminating against unreliable people."

Source: dailymail.com

 ## That Reminds Me of a Joke

When an office worker arrived at his desk at 11:00, his angry boss confronted him.

"You should have been here at nine!" said the boss.

The employee responded, "Why, what happened?"

Thou Stinks!

We think of medieval monks as suffering in silence. Wrong! They complained mercilessly, often in the margins of the texts they were transcribing.
Here are a few:

"New parchment, bad ink; I say nothing more."

"St. Patrick of Armagh, deliver me from writing."

"Now I've written the whole thing: For Christ's sake give me a drink."

Source: brainpickings.org

That Reminds Me of a Joke

A guy joins a monastery and takes a vow of silence, though he's allowed to say two words every seven years.

After the first seven years, the elders bring him in and ask for his two words.

"Cold floors," he says. They nod and send him away.

Seven more years pass. They bring him back in and ask for his two words.

"Bad food," he says. They nod and send him away.

Seven more years pass. They bring him in for his two words.

"I quit," he says.

"I'm not surprised in the least," says the head monk. "You've done nothing but complain since you got here."

Bonus Joke

The new monk is assigned to copy the old texts by hand. Noticing that he'll be copying from copies and not from the original manuscripts, he tells an elderly monk, "If there was an error in the first copy, that error would be continued in all the subsequent copies."

The elderly monk agrees and goes to the cellar with a copy to check it against the original. Hours go by and nobody sees him. Concerned, the new monk searches for him in the cellar. Hearing wailing, he finds the old monk leaning over one of the original books. Looking up, he sobs, "The word is celebrate."

I I I I I I I I I I I I I I I I I I I I I I I I I I I I I I I I I I I I I I I I I I I I I I I

At Least He Won't Take Any Lip from the Customers

A man walked into a Taco Bell in Haverstraw, New York, pulled a gun on the cashier, and grabbed the loot. But he wasn't done. He then marched into the manager's office and applied for a job. He was turned down.

Source: Lohud.com

That Reminds Me of a Joke

An applicant was filling out a job application. When he came to the question, "Have you ever been arrested?" He answered, "No."

The next question, intended for people who had answered in the affirmative to the last one, was "Why?" The applicant answered it anyway: "Never got caught."

Bonus Joke

I won't be hiring this assistant soon, even if her résumé boasts,"I'm a team player with 16 years of assassinating experience."

—Cindy Donalson

Which Job Pays More?

A correction spotted in *The New Orleans Times-Picayune:* "I am sorry to disappoint all the readers who wished to apply for the position, but New Orleans does not employ a 'sex assessor.' That was a misprint in Wednesday's column. It should have read 'tax assessor.'"

 ## That Reminds Me of a Joke

I always put a dab of perfume on my tax return. Considering what they're doing to me, I might as well get them in the mood.

—Bob Monkhouse

Ironically, That Was the Most Work He Did All Year

When Dwayne Yeager came home, he found his apartment had been ransacked and his belongings strewn all over the floor. He also reported seeing a white Honda leaving the scene. But after cops spoke with neighbors they drew a bead on the culprit—Dwayne Yeager. Yeager was spotted crawling in and out of his bedroom window and, in general, acting suspicious. Later Yeager admitted to staging the burglary for the very understandable reason that he just didn't feel like going to work that day.

Source: Baynews9.com

 ## That Reminds Me of a Joke

A man calls his boss one morning and tells him that he's staying home because he is not feeling well. "What's the matter?" he asks.

"I have a case of Butt Glaucoma," he says in a weak voice.

"What's Butt Glaucoma?"

"I can't see dragging my butt into work today."

"Is It an Emergency?" "Of Course! We're Hungry!!"

Is there anything worse than cold pizza? A South Carolina Pizza Hut deliveryman doesn't think so. The volunteer firefighter devised a plan to make sure that the pizza would arrive piping hot: He'd flash his emergency lights so traffic would pull to the side and let him pass. The police were not as impressed with his ingenuity and arrested him.

Source: *The Week*

➡ That Reminds Me of a Joke

The new CEO is determined to rid the company of all slackers. On a tour of the facilities, he notices a guy leaning on a wall. The room is full of workers and he thinks this is his chance to show everyone he means business. So the CEO walks up the guy and asks, "How much money do you make a week?"

The young guy replies, "Three hundred dollars a week."

The CEO hands the guy three hundred dollars in cash and yells, "Here's a week's pay, now get out and don't come back!"

Feeling pretty good about his first firing, the CEO looks around the room and asks, "Anyone know what that slacker did here?"

One of the other workers mutters "Yeah, he was the pizza delivery guy."

Can I Have One that Isn't Used?

A Russian man was arrested for using a toilet. Now, in all fairness, it wasn't just any toilet, it was a toilet in a store. And it wasn't just any toilet in the store, it happened to be part of the store's bathroom display. That's right, the man answered his call to nature by peeing in the middle of the store in front of the other customers. According to the Russian newspaper *Utro,* the man assumed he would be allowed to try out the products before buying them.

Source: Ananova.com

That Reminds Me of a Joke

God appears to a man and says, "Son, if you want to go to Heaven, you must give up your wicked ways. You will have to give up cigarettes, alcohol, and sex." The man agrees and a week later, God reappears and asks the man how his task is going.

The man replies, "The cigarettes and alcohol were easy, but when my wife took the meat out of the freezer, I had to make love to her right then and there."

God is angry and thunders, "We don't like that sort of thing in Heaven!"

The man nods, "They didn't like it in the grocery store, either."

You Have to Applaud His Initiative

A job applicant for the Washington State patrol was in the middle of taking a polygraph test when it was abruptly ended. Turns out, officers discovered an interesting book on the front seat of his car. Its title: *How to Beat the Lie Detector.*

Source: komonews.com

➡ That Reminds Me of a Joke

A man buys a lie detector robot that slaps people who lie. He decides to test it at dinner. He asks his son, "Son, where were you today at one o'clock?"

"At school." The robot slaps the son. "Okay, I went to the movies!"

The father asks, "Which one?"

"Batman meets Harry Potter." The robot slaps the son again. "Okay, I was watching porn!"

The father replies, *"What?* When I was your age I didn't even know that such a thing existed!" The robot slaps the father.

The mom chimes in, "Ha ha! Serves you right. After all, he is your son!" The robot slaps the mother.

▮ ▮

Best Job Marketer *Ever!*

An artist went on Craig's List with this contest aimed at potential employers: "Send me a week's worth of salary and benefits. I will keep all the checks and use all the benefits. Whoever sends me the best salary package will win two days of graphic design work!!! Good luck!"

 ## That Reminds Me of a Joke

Reaching the end of a job interview, the human resources person asked a young applicant fresh out of business school, "And what starting salary are you looking for?"

The applicant said, "In the neighborhood of $125,000 a year, depending on the benefits package."

The interviewer said, "Well, what would you say to a package of 5 weeks' vacation, 14 paid holidays, full medical and dental, company matching retirement fund to 50% of salary, and a company car leased every two years—say, a red Corvette?"

The applicant sat up straight and said, "Wow! Are you kidding?"

The interviewer replied, "Yeah, but you started it."

No, He Didn't Get the Job

A college student applied for a job at a Welsh tourist attraction. But he had one thing going against him—his email address: atleastimnotwelsh.

Source: Ananova.com

That Reminds Me of a Joke

An unemployed man applies for a minimum wage job as a janitor at Microsoft. But when HR finds out he's too poor to own a computer, and therefore an email address, they refuse to hire him.

Dejected, the man leaves. He walks past a farmers' market and sees a stand selling crates of tomatoes. He buys a crate, carries it to a busy corner and displays the tomatoes. In less than two hours he sells out. He repeats the process several times more that day, then through the week and over the course of the next month. Soon, he buys a cart, which is replaced by a truck, then a fleet of trucks—all selling his tomatoes around the country. He's working harder than ever and making more money than he could ever have dreamed.

Time passes and he decides he ought to buy life insurance. He consults an insurance adviser who asks him for his email address in order to send the final documents electronically.

When the man replies that he doesn't have time to mess with a computer and has no email address, the insurance man is stunned. "No email? No computer? No Internet? Just think where you would be today if you'd had all of that five years ago!"

"I know exactly where I'd be," snorts the man. "I'd be sweeping floors at Microsoft for $5.35 an hour."

██

He Never Did Get Along with the Spleen

A pregnant Omaha woman was fired after her boss decided that her unborn child was "hostile towards him" and carried "negative energy," which, he said, brought back memories of his own awful experience in the womb.

Source: Associated Press

That Reminds Me of a Joke

Today is Bring Your Child to Work Day—or as it's known at the iPad factory in China, Bring Your Parents to Work Day.

██

Take This Down: "AAAARRRRGGGGHHHHH!"

Coworkers of a New York City court stenographer guessed he was just having one of those days. How might anyone have guessed? When he handed in his transcript for a case, he'd typed, "I hate my job, I hate my job, I hate my job" over and over again. The man was fired for misconduct.

Source: The *New York Post*

That Reminds Me of a Joke

Two bone-weary court stenographers decided they needed a break. "I know how to get some time off," the first whispered.

"How?" asked the second.

"Watch." He jumped up on his desk, kicked out a couple of ceiling tiles, and hoisted himself up. Then swinging his legs over a metal pipe, hung upside down. Within seconds, their boss appeared. "What are you doing?" he demanded.

"I'm a light bulb," answered the first stenographer.

"I think you need some time off," said the boss. "Get out of here, and I don't want to see you back here for at least another week!"

"Yes sir," said the first stenographer. He jumped down and left.

The second stenographer started to follow him out the door.

"Where are you going?" the boss asked.

"Home," he said. "I can't work in the dark."

▪ ▪

On Second Thought, We'll Take the Train

Spotted on thisisplymouth.co.uk, this headline: "Air traffic controllers can apply for job in Braille."

That Reminds Me of a Joke

A blind man walks into a hardware store with his seeing-eye dog. Without hesitation, the man picks his dog up by its leash and spins it around over his head.

"Hey!" yells the store manager. "What are you doing?"

The blind man replies, "Just looking around."

▪ ▪

Sorry, But It's Time for My Chief Advisor's Belly Rub

Brazil is one of Colombia's biggest trading partners and a regional power. So picking an ambassador to Brazil is taken very seriously, as evidenced by the fact that the person tapped was vice-president Angelino Garzon. But Garzon turned down the post citing personal problems: his dog would not like it. "[My dog] is very hairy and the hot climate of Brasilia could harm its health," he explained. Colombia's foreign minister—obviously not a dog person—commented: "When he mentioned personal problems, you would expect something deeper than that."

Source: BBC News

 That Reminds Me of a Joke

What's the difference between a businessman and a dog?

The businessman wears a suit, the dog just pants.

This Job Stinks

In 2013, the Social Security Administration issued a letter of reprimand to an employee citing "60 documented instances" of creating a "hostile work environment" and "conduct unbecoming a federal employee" by passing gas in his office.

Source: *Washington Post*

 **That Reminds Me of a Joke**

An older worker is at his desk when he turns to his cubicle mate and whispers, "I just silently passed gas. What should I do?"

His co-worker says, "Well, for starters, you can put a new battery in your hearing aid."

Employee of the Month

A traffic cop in Sweden went above and beyond the call of duty by not letting an armed bank robbery get in the way of his performing his job. When frantic police officers responded to the scene, the traffic warden stepped up and slapped a ticket on one of the police cruisers parked illegally.

Source: thelocal.se

 ## That Reminds Me of a Joke

The local sheriff was looking for a deputy, so Gomer applied for the job.

"Okay, Gomer," says the sheriff, "what is 1 and 1?"

Gomer replied, "11."

The sheriff thought to himself, That's not what I meant, but he's right. "All right, here's another question," he said. "What two days of the week start with the letter 'T'?"

"Today and tomorrow."

He was again surprised that Gomer supplied a correct answer that he had never thought of himself.

"Now Gomer, listen carefully: Who killed Abraham Lincoln?" the sheriff asked.

Gomer thought really hard for a minute and finally admitted, "I don't know."

"Well, why don't you go home and work on that one for a while?"

So, Gomer went home, where his mother asked how the interview had gone.

"Great!" he said. "First day on the job and I'm already working on a murder case!"

health
and wellness

"The word 'aerobics' came about when the gym instructors got together and said, 'If we're going to charge $10 an hour, we can't call it jumping up and down.'"

—Rita Rudner

Too Many Irons in the Fire

Tomas Paczkowski wanted to help with the chores, so he offered to do the ironing while watching TV and drinking beer. The result: When the phone rang, he answered the iron instead. Doctors say he'll make a full recovery.

Source: web.orange.co.uk

 **That Reminds Me of a Joke**

A guy arrives at the hospital with two burned ears. "How'd it happen?" asks the nurse.

"I was ironing my shirt and the phone rang," he explains. "Instead of the phone I picked up the iron."

"How'd you burn the other ear?"

"They called back."

It Could Have Been Worse. He Might Have Listened to Celine Dion

A Dutch patient's brain implant cured his obsessive-compulsive disorder. But weirdly it spawned a new one. According to doctors, the operation caused the man to become a fanatical Johnny Cash fan. The patient, says his doctor, "listens solely to Johnny Cash."

Source: *The Week*

 That Reminds Me of a Joke :

Yo' Mama is so stupid, she thought Johnny Cash was a pay toilet.

Hold Your Breath and Count to a Million

If you see Bob Taylor drinking sugar water, eating a spoonful of mustard, or even standing on his head, don't be alarmed. The Tennessee man is just trying to stop his hiccups—the ones he's had for the past 29 years. Amazingly, it isn't even a world record. That Guinness entry belongs to Iowan Charles Osborne, who hiccupped for nearly 70 years, until he died in 1990. His bout began after he unsuccessfully tried to tackle a pig. People usually get hiccups after getting soused, not sows-ed.

Source: *International Business Times*

That Reminds Me of a Joke

A woman went to her doctor's office. She was seen by one of the new doctors, but after four minutes in the examination room, she burst out screaming and ran down the hall. An older doctor stopped her and asked what the problem was, and she explained.

The older doctor marched back to the new doctor and demanded, "What's the matter with you? Mrs. Terry is 73 years old, she has four grown children and seven grandchildren, and you told her she was pregnant?"

The new doctor smiled smugly. "Cured her hiccups."

He'd Just Watched the Movie *Marathon Man*

When police from the French village of St. Gervais stumbled upon a young boy in hiding, he told them a harrowing tale. On his way to the dentist, he said, a stranger in a neighboring town abducted him. Luckily, he escaped. The boy gave a full description of his kidnapper, including weight and height, and a full investigation was launched. A month later, the case was solved—the boy had made up the kidnapping charges because he didn't want to go to the dentist.

Source: yahoo.com

 ## That Reminds Me of a Joke

A family interrupts their vacation to go to the dentist. "I want a tooth pulled, and I don't want Novocain because I'm in a big hurry," the mother says. "Just extract the tooth as quickly as possible, and we'll be on our way."

The dentist was quite impressed. "You're certainly a courageous woman," he says. "Which tooth is it?"

The woman turns to her son and says, "Show him your tooth, dear."

Umm . . . Maybe a Knife and Fork Next Time?

You know your meal might be a tad large if you injure yourself eating it. That's what happened to a woman in Liverpool, England. She ordered a triple-layer burger, opened her mouth as wide as it would go and suddenly, pain—she had dislocated her jaw.

"The whole side of my head was hurting," she told the Press Association.

Source: web.orange.co.uk

 That Reminds Me of a Joke

Customer to friend: This is a wonderful restaurant. I ordered salad, and I got the freshest salad in the world, I ordered coffee, and I got the freshest coffee in the world.

Friend: I know—I ordered a small steak and got a calf.

I'll Drink to That

A New Zealand man went blind after downing a few shots of vodka. Denis Duthie was rushed to a hospital, where the diagnosis was formaldehyde poisoning. The cure: ethanol, which can be found in alcohol. So an employee rushed over to a liquor store and bought a bottle of whisky. It was then dripped straight into the man's stomach. "Johnnie Walker Black. It was a good whisky," said Duthie, after he could see again.

Source: web.orange.co.uk

 ## That Reminds Me of a Joke

A man goes to see the doctor, complaining of the blahs. After 20 minutes, the doctor says, "I'm sorry, but I just can't figure out what's wrong with you. It might be a result of too much alcohol."

"Don't worry about it, Doc," says the man. "I'll come back when you're sober."

—Bill Maher

Bonus Joke

Yes, alcohol kills brain cells, but it's very selective. It only kills the brain cells that contain good sense, shame, embarrassment, and restraint.

—P. J. O'Rourke

Slim Chance of These Working

Looking to lose a few pounds? Try one of these actual diets:

Sleeping Beauty Diet: If you aren't awake, you can't eat, right? Advocates sedate themselves and sleep for days.

Baby Food Diet: Babies weigh next to nothing, so it makes sense to duplicate their diet, right? In this case, replace your meals with puréed peas, fruit, carrots, chicken—whatever. Just make sure it comes in those little jars.

The Tapeworm Diet: Take one orally, or, according to tapewormdiet.net, "travel to a part of the world where beef tapeworms are endemic" and infect yourself that way.

The Cotton Ball Diet: Begin each meal with an appetizer of cotton balls. The balls will fill you up so that you won't want to eat as much.

Fletcherizing: Horace "The Great Masticator" Fletcher preached chewing each mouthful exactly 32 times until the food was "purified" and then spitting out what remained. This way, you get the nutrients with fewer calories.

Sources: listverse.com,
dietsinreview.com, everydayhealth.com

 ## That Reminds Me of a Joke

The second day of a diet is always easier than the first. By the second day you're off it.

—Jackie Gleason

Bonus Joke

Customer to waiter: I'm going to order a broiled skinless chicken breast, but I want you to bring me a lasagna and garlic bread by mistake.

—Glasbergen

The Best Rest I Ever Had

Guess who attended the funeral of Brighton Dama Zanthe in Zimbabwe? Brighton Dama Zanthe. The 34-year-old had fought illness for some time and seemed to have succumbed. But as mourners passed his coffin, the body began to move. Friends and family did what most loved ones would do under similar circumstances—they fled, fearing that he'd come back to haunt them. But, in fact, he just came back to life. Zanthe was home shortly afterwards, saying, "I feel okay."

Source: mirror.co.uk

 ## That Reminds Me of a Joke

A woman's coffin is being carried to the graveyard when it's accidentally knocked against a wall. The pallbearers hear a low moan from inside, and the casket is opened, revealing that the woman is still alive. She lives for another ten years, and when she dies her body is taken to the same graveyard. As the pallbearers approach the graveyard's entrance, the woman's husband runs toward them, shouting, "And this time, watch out for the wall!"

What a Line!

Unhappy with the direction your life is headed? Do what some Japanese are doing—have plastic surgery on your palms. The operation alters the lines on the palm, which, according to palm readers, dictate one's life. The 10-minute operation costs $10,000. One doctor said that most men wanted to change lines associated with money and business, while women seek changes to their love lines.

Source: Japan Daily Press

That Reminds Me of a Joke

Palmist: I see a fluctuation in your circumstances.
Client: What do you mean?
Palmist: Oh, just read between the lines.

Bonus Joke

A fortune-teller says to another, "What beautiful weather we're having."

"Yes," says the second. "It reminds me of the summer of 2022."

Flower Child

After watching their 16-month-old scratch at her ear for months, the Chinese parents took her to see a doctor. The doctor peered into the girl's ear canal where he had a surprise waiting for him: Growing inside was a dandelion. Apparently, a seed had lodged there and blossomed. The dandelion was surgically removed.

Source: Beijing Evening News

 That Reminds Me of a Joke

A man is sitting in an airport with a carrot sticking out of his ear. Everybody is staring, but nobody wants to say anything to him. Finally, a passenger walks up to the man and says, "Hey, buddy. You know you have a carrot in your ear?"

The man says, "WHAT? SPEAK UP. I GOT A CARROT IN MY EAR!"

One More Crunch or the Dog Gets It

A Boston-based inventor has a foolproof way to get people to exercise more: Torture. Maneesh Sethi, who once hired someone to slap him in the face every time he went on Facebook, has invented a bracelet that shocks the wearer if they fail to meet their fitness targets. "Sometimes crazy works," said Sethi.

Source: *The Week*

 ## That Reminds Me of a Joke

"I get plenty of exercise carrying the coffins of my friends who exercise."

—Red Skelton

. . . .

Oh, the Irony

When Baltimore handed out its first citation to a restaurant, it was for repeated violations of the city's trans fat ban. The name of the eatery: Healthy Choice.

Source: WBALTV

 ## That Reminds Me of a Joke

Hear about the new restaurant called Karma? There's no menu—you get what you deserve.

. . . .

I'm Not Positive, But I Think I Know Why

"Suicide Forum Sees Drop in Attendance."

Aspen (Colo.) *Daily News* headline

That Reminds Me of a Joke

"Suicide is our way of saying to God, 'You can't fire me. I quit.'"

. . . .

Sure, Big Bird Acts Nice, but . . .

A lot of people suffer from automatonophobia, the fear of puppets. But scared of the Muppets? "All it takes is for my husband, to hum the theme song and I'm a wreck," says Lindsay Broom. The 37-year-old from Swansea, England, says she's been petrified of them since she was five, when she and her mother bought a rabbit hutch from a sickly, elderly woman. "The woman sat there groaning and wheezing as she watched the Muppets," she said. "It was the most terrifying experience of my life."

Source: metro.co.uk

That Reminds Me of a Joke

I thought it was weird when my friend told me he'd
fallen in love with a puppet. Now he's planning on
marionette.

Take Two Crumbling Streets and Call Me in the Morning

Ray Lee was working out when his heart rate skyrocketed to a dangerous 190 beats per minute. An ambulance was called and the EMTs threw the 65-year-old in the back. As they sped off to a hospital, they hit a massive pothole. The impact jolted Lee's heart, dropping it back down to a healthy 60 beats per minute.

Source: shortlist.com

 That Reminds Me of a Joke

St. Peter is very busy in Heaven, so he leaves a sign by the Pearly Gates: "For Service, Ring Bell." And off he goes. He barely gets started when DING! the bell rings. He rushes back to the gates, but no one's there.

St. Peter goes back to work when suddenly DING! the bell rings again. He rushes back to the gates, but no one's there. A little annoyed, St. Peter goes back to work.

DING! There it goes. And still no one's there.

"Okay, that's it," he says. "I'm going to hide and watch to see what's going on." So St. Peter hides, and a moment later, a little old man walks up and rings the bell.

St. Peter jumps out and yells, "Aha! Are you the guy who keeps ringing the bell?"

"Yes, that's me," the little old man says.

"Well, why do you keep ringing the bell and going away?" St. Peter asks.

"They keep resuscitating me."

Bonus Joke

Two doctors and an HMO manager die and line up together at the Pearly Gates. One doctor steps up and tells St. Peter, "As a pediatric surgeon, I saved hundreds of children." St. Peter lets him enter.

The next doctor says, "As a psychiatrist, I helped thousands of people live better lives." St. Peter tells him to go ahead.

The last man says, "I was an HMO manager. I got countless families cost-effective health care."

St. Peter replies, "You may enter. But," he adds, "you can only stay for three days. After that, you can go to hell."

The Next Round's on Us

Dorothy Howe has the secret to longevity: whiskey and cigarettes. The 100-year-old Brit estimates she's smoked 460,000 cigarettes in her lifetime and chased them down with copious amounts of her favorite booze.

"My doctor said I wouldn't be alive without them," she said.

Source: The *Daily Mail*

➡ That Reminds Me of a Joke

The 98-year-old Mother Superior was dying. The nuns gathered around her bed trying to make her last journey comfortable. They gave her some warm milk to drink, but she refused. One of the nuns took the glass back to the kitchen and poured a generous amount of whiskey into the milk. Back at Mother Superior's bed, she held the glass to her lips. Mother drank a little, then a little more and before they knew it, she had drunk the whole glass down to the last drop.

"Mother," the nuns asked with earnest, "please give us some wisdom before you die."

She raised herself up in bed and with a pious look on her face said, "Don't sell that cow."

How to Make Paying Taxes Even More Painful

To increase colon cancer screenings, an Idaho doctor suggested that the county include a reminder in every tax notice. The idea was nixed. "Recommending a colonoscopy in the same envelope as the tax notice may be considered ironic," the county treasurer said.

Source: Associated Press

That Reminds Me of a Joke

A boy was playing on the street when he accidentally swallowed a coin and began to choke. His panicked mother shouts out for help, and a passerby intervenes.

"Stand back," he says, authoritatively. He proceeds to dangle the boy upside down by his feet while slapping his back three times. And out pops the coin.

"Thank you so much, doctor," says the mother.

"I'm not a doctor," says the passerby. "I work for the Internal Revenue Service."

ı ı

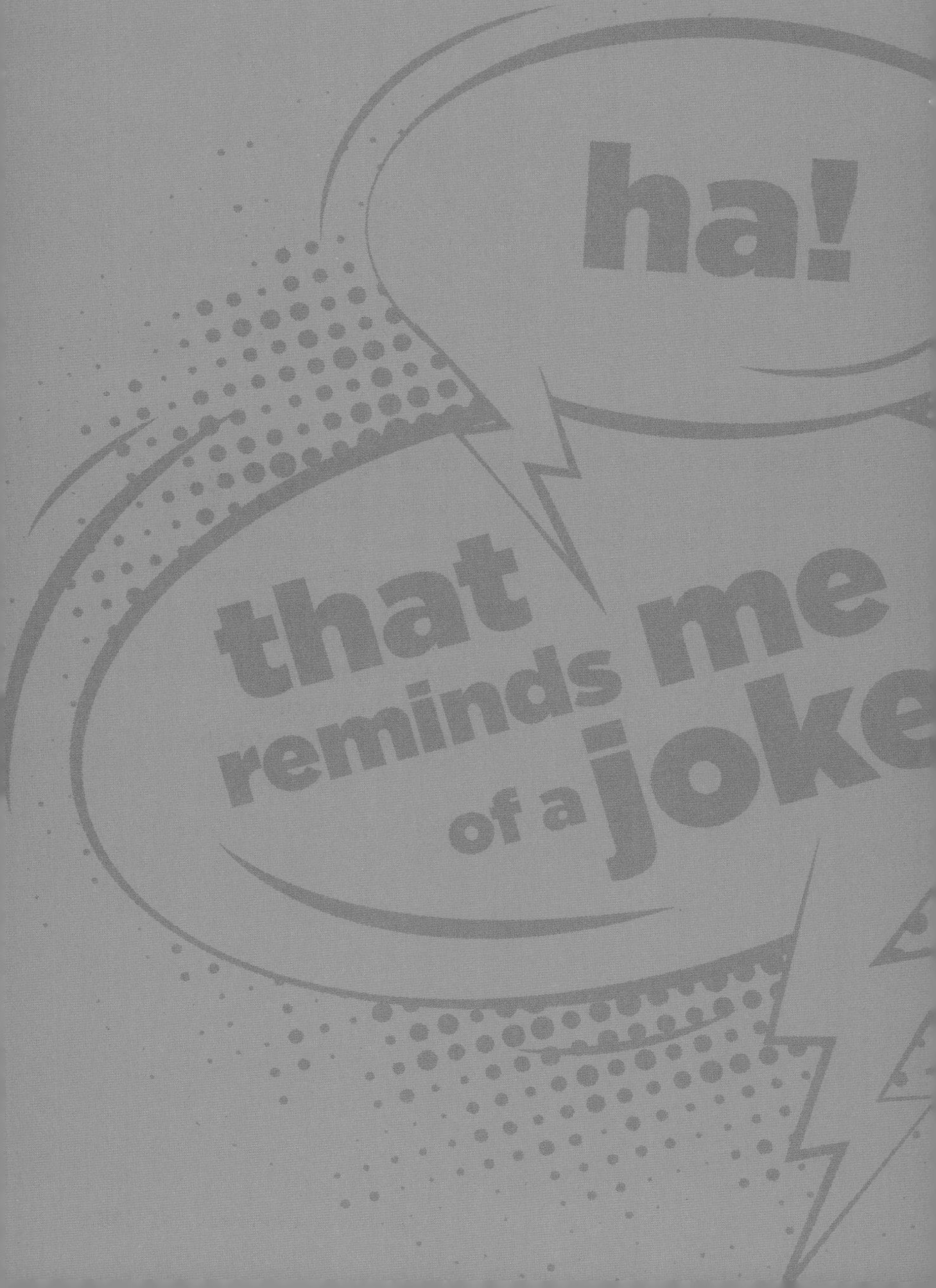
ha!
that reminds me of a joke

animal
planet

"Man is rated the highest animal,
at least among those animals
who returned the questionnaire."

—Robert Brault

It's All Going to the Birds

Tens of thousands of people packed St. Peter's Square in Vatican City to hear Pope Francis preach an end to war. The ceremony was topped by the release of two white peace doves. Clearly nonbelievers, a seagull and crow attacked the doves.

Source: Associated Press

That Reminds Me of a Joke

The peace-making meeting scheduled for today has been canceled due to a conflict.

—Purported Church Bulletin Blooper

. . . .

Now Just Slow Down

Every year, the RSPCA, the British version of the ASPCA, fields a lot of odd phone calls from distressed animal lovers. One of them: A member of the public called to report a slow moving tortoise on the shoulder of a motorway. It turned out to be a deflated football.

Source: Newspostleader.co.uk

That Reminds Me of a Joke

An extremely upset tortoise crawls into a police station.

"I've been robbed by a marauding gang of snails," **he cries to the officers.**

"Calm down," says a cop. "Just tell us everything that happened."

"That's difficult," says the tortoise. "It all happened so fast!"

Polly Wants a @#$%^* Cracker

A British pub's pet bird has a very nasty habit: She curses out the customers. Things with the African Grey reached a head when it told a bunch of clergymen exactly what it thought of them. The bird's owner, Tony Dunbar, said little Miss Pottymouth has calmed down ever since a flood closed the pub for a few months. Still, she's not the picture of feathery etiquette. Says Dunbar: she now "does a very rude gesture with her feet."

Source: hulldailymail.co.uk

 That Reminds Me of a Joke

A lonely pastor buys a parrot to keep him company. Unfortunately, the parrot curses a blue streak. The pastor yells at it to stop, but this only makes the bird swear more. Even throwing a blanket over its cage doesn't quiet it down. Furious, the pastor tosses the parrot into the freezer, and all goes quiet. Too quiet. The pastor throws open the freezer door. The parrot climbs out and humbly says, "I'm sorry for the trouble I've caused you, Father. I promise to improve my vocabulary. By the way, what did the chicken do?"

Next Year I'm Playing Hamlet!

Visitors to the wildlife park in Luohe, China, noticed something odd about the lion. How odd? It was actually a Tibetan Mastiff that zookeepers were passing off as a big cat. "I had my young son with me so I tried to play along and told him it was a special kind of lion," one mother told Orange News. The jig was up, however, when the "lion" barked.

Source: web.orange.co.uk

That Reminds Me of a Joke

I went to the zoo the other day. There was only one animal in it, a dog. It was a shih tzu.

Bonus Joke

Living in a household with eight indoor cats requires buying large amounts of kitty litter, which I usually get in 25-pound bags—100 pounds at a time. When I was going to be out of town for a week, I decided to go to the supermarket to stock up. As my husband and I both pushed shopping carts, each loaded with five large bags of litter, a man looked at our purchases and queried, "Bengal or Siberian?"

—Judy J. Hagg

And I'll Have a Side Order of Engagement Ring

When a Wisconsin woman lost her wedding ring, she was disconsolate. She searched her home high and low—nothing. Cut to five years later. Her granddaughter is eating a popsicle when her dog snatches it away and sucks it down. The popsicle didn't sit well with the dog, who threw it up. He also threw up the wedding ring, which he'd consumed five years earlier.

"Friends have said, 'I want a dog who throws up diamonds!'" she told 12newsnow.com. "Who wouldn't, right?"

That Reminds Me of a Joke

A man walks into a bar one day and asks, "Does anyone here own that Rottweiler outside?"

"Yeah, I do!" a biker says, standing up. "What about it?"

"Well, I think my Chihuahua just killed him."

"What are you talkin' about?" the biker says. "How could your little runt kill my Rottweiler?"

"Well, it seems he got stuck in your dog's throat."

Could It Be that You Bought a Hedgehog?

A distraught British woman dialed their equivalent of 911 after she bought a pet rabbit. She was inconsolable upon discovering that the rabbit didn't have floppy ears.

Source: BBC News

That Reminds Me of a Joke

Q. Why did the bunny bang his head on the piano?
A. He was playing by ear!

Bonus Gag:

Q. What's yellow, has long ears, and grows on trees?
A. The Easter Bunana!

▮ ▮

The Problem Is, He Can't See Over the Steering Wheel

Spotted in a local newspaper: "Reward! Lost black male cat (Chucky). May have gotten into vehicle & driven to other area."

That Reminds Me of a Joke

A man hated his wife's cat and decided to get rid of him by driving him 20 blocks from his home and leaving him at the park. As he arrived home, the cat was walking up the driveway.

The next day, he drove the cat 40 blocks away, booted the beast out, and headed home. Driving back up his driveway, there was the cat.

He kept taking the cat farther and farther, but the cat would always beat him home. At last he decided to drive a few miles away, turn right, then left, past the bridge, then right again and another right until he reached what he thought was a safe distance from his home and left the cat there.

Hours later the man calls home to his wife: "Jen, is the cat there?"

"Yes," the wife answers. "Why?"

"I'm lost," says the man, "and I need the cat to give me directions home."

Faster than a Speeding Pooper Scooper

The Czech Republic's newest superhero is SuperVaclav. And he has set his sights on dog owners who don't pick up after their pooch. On a video, SuperVaclav is seen picking up dog poo and pelting the dog owner with it. "His only super power seems to be running pretty fast," said an observer. "Because the dog owner is furious and sprints after him."

Source: web.orange.co. uk

 That Reminds Me of a Joke

A guy walks into the bar on the top floor of a skyscraper and orders a drink. A guy sitting near him says, "There's a nice breeze outside, and if you jump out it will blow you right back in."

"Prove it," says the second guy. So the first guy jumps out the window and comes soaring right back in.

"I bet you can't do it again." The first guy jumps out again, and, as before, the breeze takes him right back into the bar.

The second guy's sold and decides he needs to try this. He goes to the window, leaps out, and plummets to his death.

The bartender turns to the first guy and says, "You know, you're a real jerk when you're drunk, Superman."

▪▪▪

Parrot? How About Rat!

Police in Mexico City nabbed a drunken driver with the help of his pet parrot. When the driver stopped at an alcohol checkpoint, the parrot repeatedly yelled, "He's drunk! He's drunk!" The bird knew what he was talking about. Reyes failed a sobriety test and was arrested. Reyes, however, is not one to hold a grudge: The parrot was allowed to accompany him to jail.

Source: UPI

That Reminds Me of a Joke

One day, a man went to an auction and bid on a parrot. He really wanted this bird, so he got caught up in the bidding. He kept on bidding but kept getting outbid, so he bid higher and higher and higher. Finally, after he bid way more than he intended, he won the bid. The parrot was his, at last!

As he was paying for the parrot, he said to the auctioneer: "I sure hope this parrot can talk. I would hate to have paid this much for him only to find out that he can't talk!"

"Oh, he can talk," said the auctioneer. "Who do you think kept bidding against you?"

We Want to Bark with Our Lawyer!

From the Argus (Burlington, Washington) Police Blotter: "A citizen reported that about five dogs had charged at him in a menacing manner. A deputy checked the area. The deputy reported questioning the dogs in the neighborhood—they all denied involvement."

 That Reminds Me of a Joke

An Alsatian went to a telegram office, took out a blank form, and wrote, "Woof. Woof. Woof. Woof. Woof. Woof. Woof. Woof. Woof."

The clerk told the dog: "There are only nine words here. You could send another Woof for the same price."

The dog looked confused: "But that would make no sense at all."

Bonus Joke

At a workshop on dog temperament, the instructor noted that a test for a canine's disposition was for an owner to fall down and act hurt. A dog with poor temperament would try to bite the person, whereas a good dog would lick his owner's face or show concern.

Once, while eating pizza in the living room, I decided to try out this theory on my two dogs. I stood up, clutched my heart, let out a scream, and collapsed on the floor. The dogs looked at me, glanced at each other, and raced to the coffee table for my pizza.

—Susan Mottice

▪ ▪

There's a Case in the Trunk

Every year since 1992, zookeepers at Islamabad, Pakistan's Marghazar Zoo have demanded alcohol, which they fed to the zoo's elephants during mating season. Without it, they insisted, the elephants would become violent. Only recently did it dawn on anyone that elephants are teetotalers. The zookeepers were fired.

Source: tribune.com.pk

 ## That Reminds Me of a Joke

A zookeeper walks into a pub with an elephant and orders two beers. After a few hours and a few more drinks, the elephant collapses drunk on the floor. As the zookeeper stumbles toward the door, the bartender calls after him, "Hey! You can't just leave that lyin' here!"

The zookeeper slurs, "That's not a lion, it's an elephant."

▪ ▪

S-S-S-S-S-S-SURPRISE!

A Texas woman and her son were working in their yard when they were surprised by a snake. Clearly not reptile-o-philes, they decided the best way to do away with the serpent was with gasoline and a match. The flaming snake slithered into some brush, setting it aflame, which, in turn, spread to their home and destroyed it.

Source: *Texas Monthly*

That Reminds Me of a Joke

An old snake goes to see his doctor. "Doc, I need something for my eyes . . . can't see well these days."

The doctor fixes him up with a pair of glasses and tells him to return in two weeks. The snake comes back in two weeks and tells the doctor he's very depressed.

"What's the problem . . . didn't the glasses help you?" asks the doctor.

"The glasses are fine. I just discovered I've been living with a water hose the past two years."

I I I I I I I I I I I I I I I I I I I I I I I I I I I I I I I I I I I I I I I I I I I I I I

Rinse, Spin, Purr

Cats are pretty neurotic about keeping themselves clean, so there's really no need to throw them into the washing machine. Still, that's what happened to Daryl Humdy's cat, Natasha. Humdy's roommate was loading his dirty clothes into washing machine under the watchful gaze of six-month-old Natasha. When he turned away for a second, the cat jumped in. The roommate threw more clothes in, closed the lid, and turned on the machine. Thirty-five minutes later, the cat's ride was over. The roommate opened the lid, and removed his clothes, along with a shaken Natasha.

Source: nbcbayarea.com

 That Reminds Me of a Joke

What do you call a cat that's been thrown in the dryer? Fluffy.

Bonus Joke

Before I rush out to work, I give my hair a quick going over with a brush I leave on the hall table. One morning I was horrified to see my son grooming the cat with my hairbrush.

"What do you think you're doing?" I demanded.

He looked puzzled and said, "But I do this every day."

—Bonnie Gauthier

The Watch Cat Is on the Job

- **THE CALL:** A Romanian man called police to report hearing a strange noise in a house.

- **WHEN COPS ARRIVED:** They arrested the man, because he happened to be burgling the house at the time.

- **UPON FURTHER INVESTIGATION:** It turned out that the man was the only one in the house, aside from the homeowner's noisy cat.

Source: Shortlist.com

That Reminds Me of a Joke

Purranoia: the fear that the cat is up to something.

▮ ▮

Wanted: One Anthropomorphic Cat

A purr-fectly fine classified ad: "Free to good home: Young cat, speaks Spanish."

 That Reminds Me of a Joke

A mother mouse and a baby mouse are walking along, when all of a sudden a cat attacks them.

The mother mouse goes, "WOOF!" and the cat runs away.

"See?" says the mother mouse to her baby. "Now do you see why it's important to learn a foreign language?"

▪▪▪

Good Idea, but . . .

In an effort to save 80 European fallow deer from being butchered, the Animal Liberation Front cut a hole in the fence of a Molalla, Oregon, deer farm and set them free. The farm owner was dismayed. Why, he wondered, would anyone want to release tame deer during hunting season?

Source: seattlepi.com

That Reminds Me of a Joke

I like to go to concerts that are related, like Talking Heads with Simple Minds. I also rent videos together. Last week I rented *Bambi* and *The Deerhunter.*

—Mark Pitta

░░░░░░░░░░░░░░░░░░░░░░░░░░░░░░░░░░░░░░░

Man's Fickle Friend

When Dan Reierson arrived back home in East Wenatchee, Washington, he was surprised to find a stranger in his kitchen. More surprising than that, the refrigerator door was open and the man was feeding Reierson's dog. Even more surprising: As the stranger calmly headed toward the door, he called to the dog, and the two left the house together.

Source: *The Wenatchee World*

 ## That Reminds Me of a Joke

They say the dog is man's best friend. I don't believe that. How many of your friends have you neutered?

—Larry Reeb

░░░░░░░░░░░░░░░░░░░░░░░░░░░░░░░░░░░░░░░

Going Ape

Employees at a Spanish zoo conducted an emergency drill that simulated a gorilla escape. To make it more realistic, a zookeeper dressed up as an ape and took off. Unfortunately, not everyone on staff was notified about the drill. Upon seeing a fleeing "gorilla," one of the zoo veterinarians grabbed a tranquilizer gun and shot the employee in the leg.

Source: Thedodo.com

That Reminds Me of a Joke

When a zoo's gorilla dies, the zookeeper hires an actor to don a costume and act like an ape until they can get another one. In the cage, the actor makes faces, swings around, and draws a huge crowd. He then crawls across a partition and atop the lion's cage, infuriating it. But the actor stays in character, until he loses his grip and falls into the lion's cage. Terrified, he shouts, "Help! Help me!"

Too late. The lion pounces, opens its massive jaws, and whispers, "Shut up! Do you want to get us both fired?"

Bonus Joke

A man walked into his backyard one morning and found a gorilla in a tree. He called a gorilla-removal service, and soon a serviceman arrived with a stick, a Chihuahua, a pair of handcuffs, and a shotgun.

"Now listen carefully," he told the homeowner. "I'm going to climb the tree and poke the gorilla with this stick until he falls to the ground. The trained Chihuahua will then go right for his, uh, sensitive area, and when the gorilla instinctively crosses his hands in front to protect himself, you slap on the handcuffs."

"Got it," the homeowner replied. "But what's the shotgun for?"

"If I fall out of the tree before the gorilla," the man said, "shoot the Chihuahua."

—Timothy Sledge

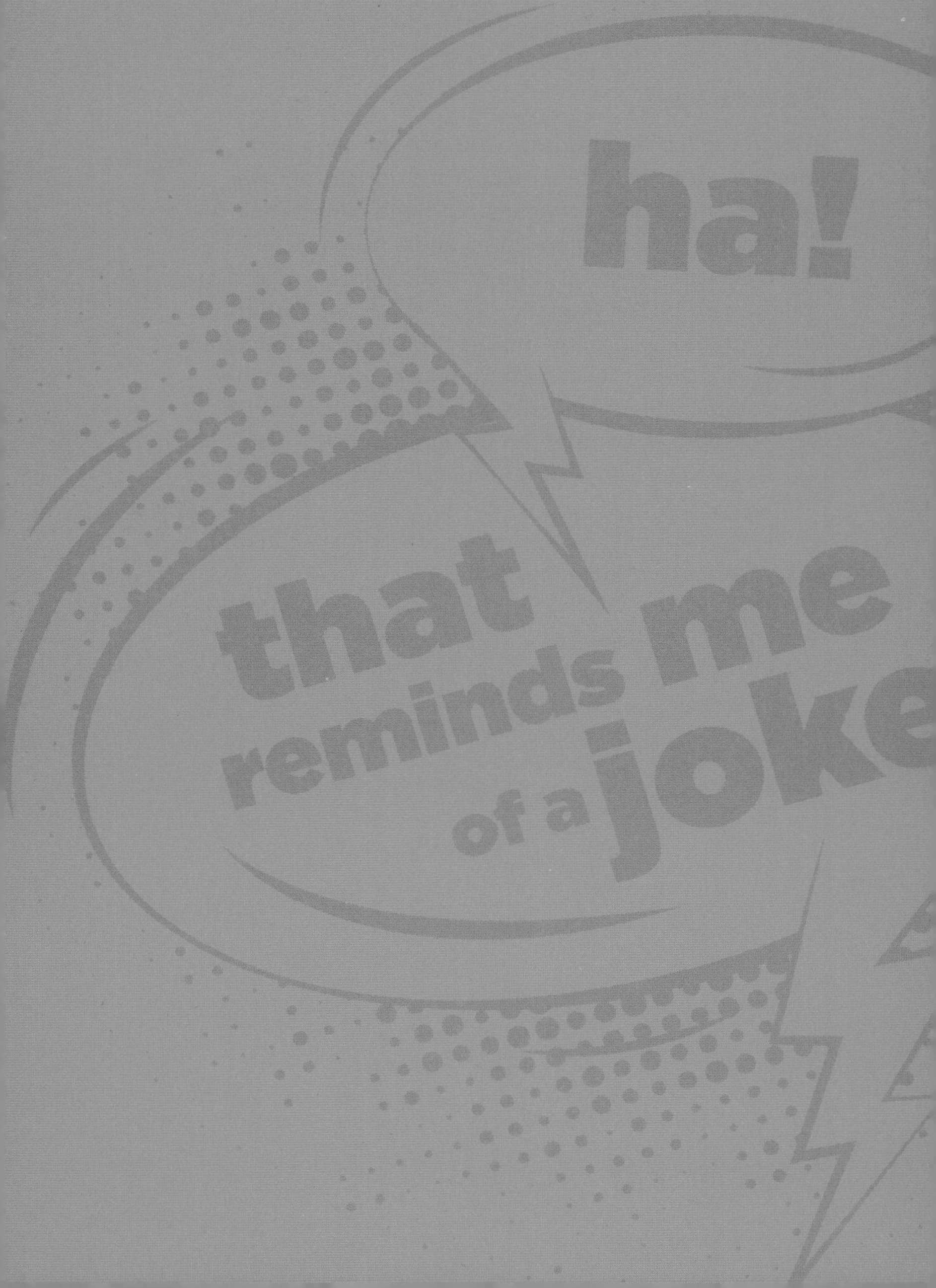
ha!
that reminds me of a joke

crime
and punishment

"I used to want to be a lawyer,
but I didn't want to have
half my brain sucked out."

—Max Walker

Congratulations! You've Won An All-Expenses-Paid Trip to Jail!

A shoplifter walked out of a store in Green Valley, California, after loading up her purse with purloined items. But before leaving, she stopped just long enough to fill out a raffle ticket, which included her full name and address. She was arrested soon after.

Source: *The Union* (Grass Valley, California)

 That Reminds Me of a Joke

A shoplifter is caught red-handed trying to steal a watch from a jewelry store. "Listen," she says, "I know you don't want any hassles either. What do you say I just buy the watch, and we forget about this?" The manager agrees and writes up the sales slip. The crook looks at the slip and says, "Hmm, this is a little more than I intended to spend. Can you show me something less expensive?"

Mooning Over You

When a British man saw a mysterious flying object that lit up the sky he immediately phoned the authorities. Before the police could react, the man called back, saying mystery solved. The UFO was actually the moon.

Source: web.orange.co.uk

 ## That Reminds Me of a Joke

Why is it that all of the instruments seeking intelligent life in the universe are pointed *away* from Earth?

Giving It Up for Lint

A Greenville, North Carolina, man was arrested after undercover cops bought 150 bags of heroin off him. Upon searching the 315-pound man, police found an additional 40 bags of heroin, crack cocaine, and Percocet pills located in a well-concealed area: his belly button.

Source: wnct.com

 ## That Reminds Me of a Joke

Q: What did the policeman say to his belly button?
A: You're under a vest!

Should Have Inked a Deal Instead

Police in Pico Rivera, California, had an easy time pinning a four-year-old murder on Anthony Garcia. That's because he pinned it on himself with an elaborate tattoo on his chest depicting the killing.

Cops noticed the incriminating ink when taking Garcia's mug shot for a petty crime. The tattoo revealed all the details of the night, from the Christmas lights and bent street lamp near the liquor store where the body was found to the image of an angry helicopter—Garcia's nickname was "Chopper"—machine-gunning the victim.

Source: breakingbrown.com

That Reminds Me of a Joke

I always look for a woman who has a tattoo. I see a woman with a tattoo, and I'm thinking, "Okay, here's a gal who's capable of making a decision she'll regret in the future."

—Richard Jenni

CSI: STUPIDVILLE

A guy in Lincoln, Nebraska, arrived home one day to find he'd been burgled—his favorite hookah pipes were missing—so he called the cops. He ended up in jail, however, after police arrived and found the pot plants he was growing.

Source: Azcentral.com

 That Reminds Me of a Joke

Three guys—a sex addict, an alcoholic, and a pothead—went to hell and stood before the devil. "I'll make a deal with you," said the devil. "I will lock you in a room with what ever you did for a thousand years, and if you get over any of your sins I will send you back to heaven."

So the sex addict got locked in a room full of beautiful women, the alcoholic got locked in a room full of beer, and the pothead locked in a room full of weed.

A thousand years later, the Devil goes to the sex addict, who staggers out saying, "I've had enough loving, I never want to see a woman again!" Poof! Off to heaven he goes.

The Devil opens the alcoholic's room. He's suffering a horrible hangover and whispers, "I'm never having another drop of beer," and off to heaven he goes.

The Devil next opens the pothead's room. The pothead comes out holding a joint and asks, "Anybody have a light?"

Guess Who Has a Fool for a Lawyer?

Philome Cesar decided to represent himself in court against charges of robbery. But his legal skills were on par with his larceny skills. During the trial, he asked a witness to describe the robber's voice. The response: "He sounded like you." Ironically, the jury's decision sounded a lot like "guilty."

Source: mcall.com

That Reminds Me of a Joke

Before a burglary trial, the judge explained to the defendant, "You can let me try your case or you can choose to have a jury of your peers."

The man thought for a moment. "What are peers?" he asked.

"They're people just like you."

"Forget it," said the defendant. "I don't want to be tried by a bunch of thieves."

Bonus Joke

As a judge, I was sentencing criminal defendants when I saw a vaguely familiar face. I reviewed his record and found that the man was a career criminal, except for a five-year period in which there were no convictions.

"Milton," I asked, puzzled, "how is it you were able to stay out of trouble for those five years?"

"I was in prison," he answered. "You should know that—you were the one who sent me there."

"That's not possible," I said. "I wasn't even a judge then."

"No, you weren't the judge," the defendant countered, smiling mischievously. "You were my lawyer."

—Philip R. Riley

ı ı

The Gun Was Probably Fake, Too

During a stickup, a bank robber in Phoenix told the teller to hand over "all the twenties, forties, and sixties."

Source: Phoenix *Times-Herald*

 That Reminds Me of a Joke

A big-city counterfeiter decided the best place to pass off his phony $18 bills would be in some small hick town. So he got into his new wheels and off he went, stopping in a tiny town with a single store. He entered the store and handed one of the bogus bills to the man behind the counter. "Can you change this for me, please?" he said.

"Ah reckon so," said the store clerk. "Ya want two nines or three sixes?"

Bonus Joke

My cousin was behind the bakery's cash register one morning when a gunman burst in and demanded all the cash. As she nervously handed over the money, she noticed the rolls of coins in the back of the register. "Do you want the rolls too?" she asked.

"No," said the robber, waving his gun. "Just the money."

—Phil Leman

Lost on A-peel

According to the bus driver, it was a brutal, unprovoked attack. A woman got on his bus and assaulted him with a half-eaten banana. "I had banana all over me," he insisted. "On my tie, my shirt, and my eye."

The woman explained that the driver almost hit her car, and that when she entered the bus to rationally discuss the matter, the banana slipped . . . right into his tie, his shirt, his eye . . .

The court may not have believed that, but it did believe her when she argued that it was "unreasonable that a banana could cause this much damage." They slapped her with only a $100 fine.

Source: thelocal.se

 ## That Reminds Me of a Joke

I feel stupid when I write the word banana. Its like, how many na's are on this thing? 'Cause I'm like "Bana . . . keep going. Banananana . . . damn."

—Demetri Martin

▪ ▪

What's in a Name?

Police officers in Bethel, Connecticut, pulled over a car after it was driving erratically. Inside, they found marijuana and two brothers: Gregory and Timothy Weed.

Source: Danbury *News Times*

The Victorville, California, bomb squad was called to a house to remove a 500-pound bomb capable of wiping out everything in the vicinity. Cops arrested the homeowner, David S. Bangs.

Source: Victorville *Daily Press*

A Chesapeake, Virginia, man was arrested after failing a breathalyzer test. The man, who blew a 0.230 on the test—three times higher than the legal limit—was Randy Joe Beverage.

Source: tampabay.com

A Houston man was arrested after authorities claimed he practiced law without a license. The 43-year-old's name: Perry Mason.

Source: youngtexaslawyer.com

 ## That Reminds Me of a Joke

A mother was sitting on the couch reading a book when one of her children walked up to her and said, "Mommy, why is my name Petal?"

The mother replied, "Because when you were born, a petal fell on your head."

The next child walked up and asked, "Mommy, why is my name Rose?"

She replied, "Because when you were born, a rose fell on your head."

The last child walked up to her and said, "BLAS CLAFLAS YIFRASSAM TASSM POONNFFFIINRTY."

The mother replied, "Please be quiet, Refrigerator."

Go Back to Sleep

A student staying at a hotel had an early morning exam the next day, and she asked the front desk to wake her up in time. It didn't happen. So she slapped a $6,000 lawsuit against the hotel for not waking her up. The lawsuit was thrown out, however, when the plaintiff slept through her court date.

Source: croatiantimes.com

 That Reminds Me of a Joke

"I was staying at a hotel and I asked for a wake-up call. The next morning the phone rang and someone said, "What are you doing with your life?"

—Demetri Martin

Hair Today, Jail Tomorrow

A Hackettstown, New Jersey, man was charged with aggravated assault by police after attacking his friend following an argument. Their disagreement? Which one had the more hirsute behind.

Source: Easton (Pennslyvania) *Express-Times*

 That Reminds Me of a Joke

Once there was a woman who bought a house. She wanted to name it, so she said, "The next thing I hear I will name my house!" She went down the street, and the first thing she heard was "hairy butt."

Then she went and bought a dog and said, "The next thing I hear I'll name the dog." The next thing she heard was "huge zit."

The next day, her dog ran away, so she went to the police station, crying.

"What's wrong?" asked the desk sergeant.

She sobbed, "I looked all around my hairy butt, but I can't find my huge zit anywhere!!!"

Naked Ambition

A Tennessee man was arrested for streaking through a Tennessee supermarket. When police asked him why he'd gone shopping sans clothing, he replied, "I was bored and didn't have anything else to do."

Source: Aolnews.com

That Reminds Me of a Joke

Two old men were sitting on a park bench outside the local town hall where a flower show was in progress. One of the men said, "Life is so boring. We never have any fun anymore. For five dollars I'd take my clothes off right now and streak through that stupid flower show!"

"You're on!" said the other old man holding up a five dollar bill. As fast as he could, the first old man fumbled his way out of his clothes and, completely naked, streaked through the front door of the flower show. Waiting outside, his friend soon heard a huge commotion inside the hall, followed by loud applause. The naked man burst out through the door surrounded by a cheering crowd.

"What happened?" asked his waiting friend.

"I won first prize for Best Dried Arrangement!"

Her Next Vehicle? A Lawn Mower

A woman in Dacula, Georgia, contacted police when her Chevy van went missing. Before the police could respond, she called back to report that the vehicle had been found. It was in her yard, hidden behind tall weeds.

Source: dacula.patch.com

 **That Reminds Me of a Joke**

You might be a redneck if you've ever cut your grass and found a car.

—Jeff Foxworthy

▮ ▮

If She Took a Shower Once in a While, She Might Know These Things

After Elaine Owens saw a red glow in her trailer's bathroom, she called 911 to report a fire. When firemen showed up, they discovered that the flames were actually sunlight reflected off the shower curtain.

Source: theworldlink.com

 That Reminds Me of a Joke

I thought I wanted to become a fireman. But as it turns out, I just like breaking windows with axes.

—Buzz Nutley

▮ ▮

aye-aye-ayePhone

A San Francisco thief pedaled his bike up to a woman on the sidewalk, snatched the iPhone out of her hands, and rode away. Unknown to him, the woman was in the middle of demonstrating the iPhone's new GPS tracking device, which worked—the thief was captured minutes later.

Source: sfgate.com

 ## That Reminds Me of a Joke

There's a new trend of people calling "Find My iPhone" to confront thieves who have stolen their iPhone. They use the app "Find My iPhone" to find the thief. And this explains the app called "Find My Stupid Friend Who Went After the Criminal Who Stole My iPhone." Way to get murdered.

—Conan O'Brien

High Inflation

According to a recent study, 90% of American paper money contains traces of cocaine. This may have come about through drug deals, using the bills to snort the powder, or via contaminated bank counting machines.

"When I was a kid, my mom told me the dirtiest thing in the world is money," said the researcher, Yuegang Zuo, professor of chemistry and biochemistry at the University of Massachusetts, Dartmouth. "Mom is always right."

Source: CNN

That Reminds Me of a Joke

Q: What happened after the government released a survey finding that most US currency is laced with cocaine?

A: The street value of a dollar bill jumped to $1.14.

Bonus Joke

Money doesn't talk, it swears.

—Bob Dylan, "It's Alright Ma (I'm Only Bleeding)"

▮ ▮

Tell Him It's Harder to Escape in High Heels

With thousands of dollars in debt and bailiffs on her tail, a Russian woman named Natalya was at her wit's end. So she did what any reasonable person would do under similar circumstances: She had a sex-change operation. "Andrian" got a new passport and even managed to borrow more money. But he can't get off that easily, said authorities. "If a debtor thinks he can escape that way, he's very much mistaken," said a spokeswoman for the Russian bailiffs.

Source: dailystar.co.uk

That Reminds Me of a Joke

Q: What's the most common crime committed by transvestites?

A: Male fraud.

. . . .

Let Me See, Have I Forgotten Anything?

After Andrew Bawden posted bail, Australian police picked him up on two counts of burglary when they found his police charge sheet at the first burgled home and a DVD of his interrogation at the second.

Source: Brisbane (Australia) *Courier Mail*

That Reminds Me of a Joke

A man went to the police station wishing to speak with the burglar who had broken into his house the night before.

"You'll get your chance in court," said the desk sergeant.

"No, no, no!" said the man. "I need to speak to him now! I want to know how he got into the house without waking my wife. I've been trying to do that for years!"

▮ ▮

Stop, in the Name of the Lie!

A man was impersonating a police officer when he pulled over another car for speeding. The driver quickly sussed out that the faux cop was fibbing since he, too, was a cop, but in his case, the kind of cop who doesn't have to pretend he's a cop because he really is a cop. The man was arrested for impersonating a police office.

Source: abcnews.go.com

 ## That Reminds Me of a Joke

I lied on my CV. I said I worked for the CIA, and they'll never find out I'm lying. When they ask what it was like working there, all I need to reply with is, "I'm not allowed to say."

Dudheads

A Los Angeles attorney sued another attorney who had hung a cardboard tombstone in his office that read "R.I.P./Jerry Garcia (a few too many parties perhaps?)." The plaintiff lawyer, a Garcia fan, alleged this joke caused him "humiliation, mental anguish, and emotional and physical distress." He further added that he had suffered injury to his mind and body (specifics were not listed in the suit).

Source: realpolice.net

That Reminds Me of a Joke

Jerry Garcia comes to his senses right after his death, looks around, and sees that he is in the midst of rock music's late great ones: Jimi Hendrix, Janis Joplin, Elvis Presley, and many more. So Jerry walks up to Jimi and says, "This is fantastic, man! I never thought heaven would be like this, spending all of eternity playing music with all the great ones!"

Jimi looks at Jerry and says, "What? You mean you think you're in heaven?"

Just then, Karen Carpenter appears on stage, takes the microphone, and says, "Alright now, one more time until you get it right: 'Close to you.'"

But the Sentence Was Real

A California woman facing five years in jail for forging drug prescriptions brought a doctor's note to court that suggested her case be postponed for medical reasons. Her request was rejected—the doctor's note was a forgery.

Source: Yahoo News

 ### That Reminds Me of a Joke

A woman goes to the pharmacist and handed him her prescription. The pharmacist said, "I can't accept this, it's a forgery."

"Why do you think it's a forgery?" asked the woman.

"Because I can read it."

▪▪

No, Honest, I Have a Bridge to Sell You

Consumers in northern Alabama became suspicious when they received recorded messages urging them call a phone number where they could "update" their bank account records. Their caller IDs read: "This is a scam."

Source: enewscourier.com

That Reminds Me of a Joke

A customer at Green's Gourmet Grocery marvels at the proprietor's intelligence.

"Tell me, Green, what makes you so smart?"

"I wouldn't share my secret with just anyone," Green replies, lowering his voice so the other shoppers won't hear. "But since you're a good and faithful customer, I'll let you in on it. Fish heads. You eat enough of them, you'll be positively brilliant."

"You sell them here?" the customer asks.

"Only four dollars apiece," says Green.

The customer buys three. A week later, he's back in the store complaining that the fish heads were disgusting and he isn't any smarter.

"You didn't eat enough." says Green. The customer goes home with 20 more fish heads. Two weeks later, he's back and this time he's really angry.

"Hey, Green," he says, "you're selling me fish heads for four dollars a piece when I can buy the whole fish for two dollars. You're scamming me!"

"You see?" says Green. "You're smarter already."

▪ ▪

Taking a Powder

For a trio of drug thieves, it was their lucky day. They broke into a house in Silver Springs, Florida, and discovered three jars of cocaine. They took them home and snorted the contents. That's when they discovered that the jars were in fact urns and they were snorting the cremains of the victim's husband and two dogs.

Source: myfoxdfw.com

That Reminds Me of a Joke

My grandpa swore by adding a spoonful of gunpowder to his tea every morning. He said that it was a very old remedy to help him live longer, and it worked: He lived to the ripe old age of 97. He left a widow, two children, fourteen grandchildren, and a fifty-foot crater where the crematorium used to be.

A Whole New Meaning for "Legal Briefs"

A Minnesota lawyer agreed to handle a woman's divorce case. One thing led to another and the two began having an affair. The tryst didn't last long, and the two parted ways romantically and professionally. But not before the lawyer submitted his bill to her, which included time they spent in court as well as in bed. The attorney had his law license suspended for 15 months.

Source: twinscities.com

That Reminds Me of a Joke

A lawyer emailed a client: Dear Jennifer, thought I saw you on the street the other day. Crossed over to say hello, but it wasn't you, so I went back. One-tenth of an hour: $30.

Bonus Joke

"How much do you charge?" a man asked a lawyer.

"I get $50 for three questions," the lawyer answers.

"That's awfully steep, isn't it?" says the man.

"Yes, it is," replies the lawyer. "Now, what's your final question?"

DWI—Driving While an Idiot

SCENE: A criminal trial

LAWYER: Trooper, when you stopped the defendant, were your red-and-blue lights flashing?

WITNESS: Yes, sir.

LAWYER: Did the defendant say anything when she got out of her car?

WITNESS: She said, "What disco am I at?"

Source: rockwallheraldbanner.com

That Reminds Me of a Joke

As I pulled into a crowded parking lot, I asked the cop standing there, "Is it all right to park here?"

"No," he said. "Can't you see that No Parking sign?"

"What about all those other cars in there?"

He shrugged. "They didn't ask."

—Arthur Clum

Bonus Joke

My mom drove cross-country to visit me in college. Heading south from Tucson, we were on our way to spend the day in Mexico when a state trooper pulled us over. "What seems to be the problem?" Mom asked.

"Drug smugglers use this road a lot," he explained, "and a suspicious-acting Buick with Pennsylvania plates has been spotted going up and down it."

"I just got in yesterday," Mom said. "And I'm hardly a smuggler. Just a teacher on sabbatical.

The patrolman eyed her suspiciously. "Do you have a prescription for that?"

—Joseph Blumberg

▪ ▪

And to Prove the Point...

An Australian man was ordered to pony up $500 in court costs after he lost his lawsuit against his ex-wife. He'd taken her to court hoping the judge would order her to remove this bumper sticker from her car: "Men are idiots. I divorced the king!"

Source: news.com.au

That Reminds Me of a Joke

Q: You know why Adam and Eve had an ideal marriage?

A: He didn't have to hear about all the men she could have married. She didn't have to hear about the way his mother cooked.

∎∎

Hold the Cactus!

A Miami diner ordered the grilled artichoke special from the restaurant's menu and ended up in the hospital with stomach pains. He's now suing the restaurant, Houston's, for not warning him that he shouldn't eat the artichoke's tough, pointy leaves.

Source: foodanddrinkdigital.com

That Reminds Me of a Joke

Knock Knock.

Who's there?

Artichokes.

Artichokes, who?

Artichokes when he eats too fast!

Why They're Criminals and Not Rocket Scientists

Police raided a North Portland, Oregon, home and confiscated drugs, a sawed-off shotgun, and materials for creating methamphetamines. The homeowners themselves tipped off the cops after they posted fliers around the neighborhood advertising "Heroin for sale."

Source: kgw.com

 That Reminds Me of a Joke

I bought shoes from a drug dealer. Not sure what he laced them with, but I've been tripping all day!

It's Like the Olive Garden, Only Better

In the case of Trice v. Reynolds, an ex-chef who was serving time in an Oklahoma penitentiary sued the prison over two gripes:

1) the food was terrible, and
2) he wanted larger portions.

 **That Reminds Me of a Joke**

Three prisoners broke out of their cells and instigated a failed prison riot. After they were caught, the warden asked why they had revolted. "Warden," said one of the men. "We rebelled because the food is awful."

"I see," said the warden. "And what did you use to break the bars?"

The spokesman replied, "Oatmeal cookies."

Legal Eagles

When a man found a dead mouse in his can of Mountain Dew, he did what most people in his situation do—he spat it out. Then he sued, the other thing most of us would do. But company lawyers offered this novel—if not stomach-churning—defense: The rodent could not have originated from the bottling plant because "the mouse would have dissolved in the soda had it been in the can from the time of its bottling until the day the plaintiff drank it." Can someone pass us a glass of water?

Source: *Madison County Record* (Wisconsin)

That Reminds Me of a Joke

Why do behavioral scientists prefer lawyers to rats for their experiments?

There are some things even a rat won't do.

▪▪

And Here's the Kicker

On her way home from having dinner and drinks, Melanie Shaker of Chicago got angry with her husband and tried to kick him. Instead, she crashed through the window of a beauty salon, suffering several deep cuts. So naturally she sued the salon. Part of her argument: The store's plate glass window, which fronts a sidewalk "frequently traveled by intoxicated pedestrians," should have been stronger.

Source: wbbm780.com (Chicago)

 That Reminds Me of a Joke

A lawsuit is like a saxophone. Everyone is happy when the case is closed.

Numbers Gamed

A Fort Lee, New Jersey, woman is suing WABC-TV in New York for broadcasting the wrong winning lottery numbers. Rakel Daniele experienced the thrill of victory when the station called out her numbers, only to feel the agony of defeat days later when she learned the TV station was mistaken. Broadcasting the wrong numbers, she claimed in her suit, went "beyond all possible bounds of decency" and was "utterly intolerable in a civilized community."

Source: northjersey.com

That Reminds Me of a Joke

I've done the calculation and your chances of winning the lottery are identical whether you play or not.

—Fran Lebowitz

Caution: Stupid Labels Ahead

One can never be too safe, hence these bizarre warning labels found on everyday items.

- **ON A GLOBE:** Warning—These globes should not be referred to for navigation.

- **ON A KIDS' NECK PILLOW:** Warning— Keep product away from infants and children.

- **ON AN ELECTRIC SKILLET:** Warning— Griddle surface may be hot during and after cooking.

- **ON ELECTRIC RAZOR:** Warning—Never use while sleeping.

From Center for America

 That Reminds Me of a Joke

Some more warning labels you should be aware of:

- **GOOGLE:** Warning! You may actually find more than what you're looking for.

- **BLOGS:** May cause drowsiness.

- **APPLE COMPUTERS:** Warning! High Smug Advisory.

- **WIKIPEDIA:** Warning label does not exist. Would you like to create warning label?
- **ITUNES:** Be alert for shifting music industry paradigms.
- **MATCH.COM:** Contents may just be settling.

Close Enough

Found in a court transcript:

LAWYER: Doctor, did you say he was shot in the woods?

DOCTOR: No. I said he was shot in the lumbar region.

Source: tripod.com

 That Reminds Me of a Joke

A lawyer was walking down the street and saw an auto accident. He rushed over, started handing out business cards, and said, "I saw the whole thing. I'll take either side."

So *That's* What That Means

After her divorce was final, a British woman was still unhappy, so she sued her lawyers. Why? For neglecting to tell her that divorce would result in her marriage ending. Charges were dismissed.

Source: independent.co.uk

That Reminds Me of a Joke

A judge was interviewing a woman regarding her pending divorce. He asked, "What are the grounds for your divorce?"

She replied, "About four acres and a nice little home in the middle of the property with a stream running by."

"No," he said, "I mean, what is the foundation of this case?"

"It is made of concrete, brick, and mortar."

"I mean, what are your relations like?"

"I have an aunt and uncle living here in town, and so do my husband's parents."

"Do you have a real grudge?"

"No, we have a two-car carport and have never really needed one."

"Please," the judge tried again, "is there any infidelity in your marriage?"

"Yes, both my son and daughter have stereo sets.

We don't necessarily like the music, but the answer to your question is yes."

"Ma'am, does your husband ever beat you up?"

"Yes, about twice a week he gets up earlier than I do."

Finally, in frustration, the judge asked, "Lady, why do you want a divorce?"

"Oh, I don't want a divorce," she replied. "My husband does. He says he can't communicate with me."

▪▪▪

Say ... Geez!

A Georgia woman didn't like her police mug shot. So upon being released from jail, the Georgian called 911 to register a complaint. That led to her being arrested again, this time for misusing the 911 system. By all accounts, her second mug shot was far better.

Source: The Smoking Gun

That Reminds Me of a Joke

What do you call it when a prisoner takes her own mug shot?

A cellfie.

▪▪▪

Everything but the Kitchen Sink

A Chicago man was stopped at a red light. Next to him was a police cruiser. The man leaned over and asked if he was wanted by the police. The cops got out of their cruiser to chat with him. That's when they smelled the sweet aroma of marijuana wafting out from the driver's car. That's also when they noticed the butt of a handgun tucked into the driver's seat. Further investigation revealed an illegal loaded assault rifle, unregistered weapons, and ammunition.

So the answer to his question: Yes.

Source: *Chicago Tribune*

 ## That Reminds Me of a Joke

A man was pulled over for speeding, and the officer asked to see his driver's license and registration.

"Well, officer, I don't have a license," said the man. "It was taken away for a DUI."

"Do you have a registration for the vehicle?" asked the officer.

"No. The car isn't mine. I stole it. But I'm pretty sure I saw the registration in the glove compartment when I put the gun in it."

"There's a gun in the glove compartment?"

"Yes, sir. I used it to kill the car's owner before I stuffed her in the trunk."

The officer steps away and calls for backup. Ten minutes later, his sergeant arrives. He asks the man for his driver's license and registration. The man said, "Yes, officer, here it is."

It all checked out, so the sergeant said, "Is there a gun in the glove compartment, sir?"

The man laughs as he opens the glove compartment to show him that there's no gun. The sergeant asks him to open the trunk, because he had reason to believe that there was a body in it. The man agrees and opens the trunk: no dead body.

"Sir, I don't understand," said the sergeant. "My colleague said you didn't have a license, the car was stolen, there was a gun in the glove compartment, and a dead body in the trunk."

The man rolls his eyes and says, "I bet he said I was speeding, too."

I I I I I I I I I I I I I I I I I I I I I I I I I I I I I I I I I I I I I I I I I I I I

Also Available
from Reader's Digest

Funny Family Jokes

A famous sociologist once declared, "Boy, families are funny!" And we couldn't agree more. This collection of hilarious anecdotes, one-liners, pointed wit, and jokes shows families for what they really are—our chief source of amusement.

ISBN 978-1-62145-189-1 • $9.99 paperback

Laughter Really Is the Best Medicine

Guaranteed to put laughter in your day, this side-splitting compilation of jokes pokes fun at the facts and foibles of daily routines. This little volume is sure to tickle your funny bone.

ISBN 978-1-60652-204-2 • $9.95 paperback

Laughter Still Is the Best Medicine

According to doctors and scientific researchers, laughter can reduce stress, lower blood pressure, boost the immune system, and even protect your heart. This hilarious collection offers up some of the funniest moments that get us through our day, with jokes, gags, and cartoons that will have readers laughing out loud.

ISBN 978-1-62145-137-2 • $9.99 paperback

For more information, visit us at RDTradePublishing.com
E-book editions are also available.

Reader's Digest books can be purchased through
retail and online bookstores.